SCAFFOLDING The **Primary Comprehension Toolkit**
for **English Language Learners**

Previews and Extensions to Support Content Comprehension

GRADES K–2

Anne Goudvis

Stephanie Harvey

Brad Buhrow

Anne Upczak-Garcia

*first*hand

HEINEMANN

DEDICATED TO TEACHERS™

DEDICATED TO TEACHERS™

*first*hand
An imprint of Heinemann

Heinemann
361 Hanover Street
Portsmouth, NH 03801–3912
www.heinemann.com

Offices and agents throughout the world

"Dedicated to Teachers" is a trademark of Greenwood Publishing Group, Inc.

The authors and publisher wish to thank the students of Columbine Elementary School, Boulder, CO, for generously allowing us to showcase their work.

Editor: Tina Miller
Design and production: Eclipse Publishing Services
Text illustration: students of Columbine Elementary School
Cover design: Jenny Jenson Greenleaf
Cover photo: David Stirling

Library of Congress Cataloging-in-Publication Data
CIP data is on file with the Library of Congress

ISBN-13: 978-0-325-02847-7
ISBN-10: 0-325-02847-8

Printed in the Unites States of America

16   15   14   13   ML   2   3   4   5

Contents

To our editor, Tina Miller,
who believed in this project from the get-go
and whose thoughtful guidance and organizational genius
made it all happen

Introduction

Children are active, curious learners, so we create environments that engage kids, encourage them to investigate their world, and foster the skills and strategies they need to become independent readers, writers, and thinkers. This book supports teachers using *The Comprehension Toolkits* to make content information and thinking strategies more comprehensible for children who come from varying cultural and linguistic backgrounds and are learning English as a new language. A companion to the *The Primary Comprehension Toolkit*, this resource embodies teaching practices that encourage students learning English to become enthusiastic, thoughtful, critical readers. We set a high comprehension bar for all kids. Learning, as we define it, is all about ways to use comprehension and thinking strategies as tools to acquire content knowledge and actively use it. For an extensive body of research that supports explicit instructional practices in comprehension and thinking strategies see *The Primary Comprehension Toolkit* Teacher Guide, pages 65–68.

    Scaffolding The Primary Comprehension Toolkit *for English Language Learners* provides children learning English with the language and conceptual tools to read for understanding and express their thoughts and ideas. There is a misconception that first children need to learn English and only then can they concentrate on reading to learn content knowledge. This resource takes the opposite approach: Kids learn English and content knowledge simultaneously. They engage with texts and visuals on many topics that spark thinking as they read, view, talk, draw, and write about substantive information and ideas from the get-go. Together, *The Primary Comprehension Toolkit* and this resource ensure that children build their background knowledge and confidently use thinking and learning strategies even as they learn a new language.

All Students Can Think:
Providing "High Challenge and High Support"

Gibbons (2009) cites evidence that all too often children learning English receive "low level drill and practice activities," rather than experiencing intellectually interesting, cognitively challenging instruction. Studies have shown that English learners need daily opportunities to use creative thinking, make sense of information and ideas, ask questions, engage in research and inquiry, and "construct their own understandings through participating in substantive conversations" (Commins 2011; Gibbons 2009). Immersing students in a rich curriculum that values thinking and understanding over memorization and rote learning is the best way we know to encourage children to develop their identities as eager, curious learners—aware of the power of their own ideas, insights, and thinking.

Comprehension instruction in the *Toolkits* lays a foundation of thinking so that students internalize ways to comprehend what they read and apply strategies in their own independent reading and learning. Moreover, children learning a new language thrive in inclusive classrooms that encourage active literacy throughout the day and across the year. An environment that values diversity and welcomes children from different cultures who may speak many languages is one that most fully supports students to develop the language and learning skills necessary for school and life (Thomas and Collier 1999). Students learning English need carefully designed instruction that weaves together content knowledge and the new language they are learning in what Gibbons (2009) calls a "high challenge, high support" environment. We believe that children are most likely to become engaged, competent readers and learners when they experience high expectations and a challenging comprehension curriculum in a child-centered, vibrant, creative classroom.

Putting *Toolkit* instructional principles into practice means that students read, view, and listen to engaging texts; think deeply about them; interact with others; and acquire knowledge (Goudvis and Harvey 2005). To do this, Allington (2009) suggests that students:

- spend large amounts of time reading and thinking in texts they can and want to read.

- have extensive opportunities to respond to their reading through talking, writing, and drawing.

- view reading as a meaningful activity that is personally fulfilling.

- focus on big ideas, issues, and concepts across disciplines.

- receive explicit instruction in using strategies as tools for comprehension.

These characteristics are integral to each and every *Toolkit* lesson as well as the supporting sessions for English language learners included in this resource.

But, of course, setting the bar high comes with the responsibility to provide "high" support, which is just what *Scaffolding* The Primary Comprehension Toolkit *for English Language Learners* does. *Scaffolding*, in the Vygotskian sense of the term, is specific, focused support that "assists learners to move toward new skills, concepts or levels of understanding" (Gibbons 2002). The small-group sessions for English learners in this resource, and the *Toolkit* lessons as well, focus on language both as a way to develop, organize, and articulate ideas so as to communicate them and as a means for teachers and children to "think and learn together" (Mercer, in Gibbons 2002). Our teaching language, as we say, becomes the children's learning language. In this resource, language is the vehicle teachers and children use as they make meaning by speaking, listening, reading, writing, and creating visual representations. Highly supportive instruction in these lessons emphasizes:

- surrounding children with visuals, images, actions, and talk, which they then use to construct their own understandings.

- using focused instruction with content concepts and vocabulary as well as comprehension strategies to support kids to move toward independence.

- scaffolding students so that they transfer their ways of thinking and knowledge in their home language into English.

- linking reading and thinking strategies to appropriate language structures and frames so that children draw, talk about, and write about their new learning and content knowledge in English.

- providing intensive language practice to integrate oral and written English conventions into ongoing literacy instruction.

For children learning English, this supportive scaffolding takes place in sessions both before (the Preview) and after (Extensions) the whole-group *Toolkit* lesson (see the user's guide section below).

Learning Can't Wait: Scaffolding Conceptual Development and Building Knowledge

Children use many pathways—concrete experiences; interacting with visuals, texts, and artifacts; and lots of talk and discussion—to build their understanding and knowledge of the world. Comprehension is about so much more than the words on the page. As children learn a new language, they build their conceptual understandings of text "through purposeful talk, viewing, and creating images, hands-on experiences, and, of course, reading." Commins (2011) suggests that what makes a difference for English learners is how information is presented and how students are given access to the ideas in texts and materials. This means unpacking concepts and ways of thinking that native speakers of English may take for granted: for instance, how to ask and articulate questions or how to activate and express background knowledge that furthers understanding during reading.

Honoring the language(s), ideas, and experiences that children bring to school provides a springboard to launch them into new learning. Commins (2011) notes, "The key in a linguistically diverse environment is that teachers always mediate understanding by building the conceptual understandings in the text through visual imagery and oral discussion, not just the written word." Viewing photographs, images, maps, and diagrams and engaging in lots of discussion surrounding it all build children's "conceptual reservoir." This is Commins's term for students' store of experiences and knowledge that helps them access and understand both the world around them and the academic language demands they encounter in school. Ideally, students build this conceptual reservoir in both their home, or heritage, language *and* the language they are in the process of learning. For us, biliteracy (or even tri-literacy!) is the gold standard—so that children become ever more literate and accomplished in their home language as well as in English. The goal of this resource, however, is to share practices that teachers working primarily in English can use to make learning in a new language accessible, comprehensible, and engaging for students.

Toolkit instruction is all about acquiring and using knowledge. When students think about the content they are learning, facts and information become knowledge, which in turn builds a strong foundation for future learning.

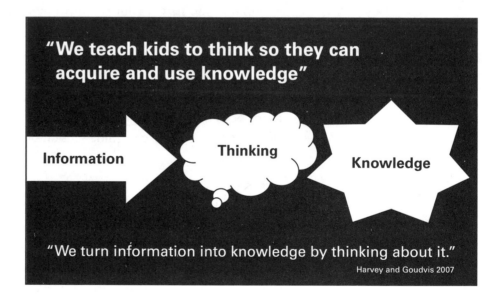

P. David Pearson's idea—Today's new knowledge is tomorrow's background knowledge—underlies the importance of "reading to learn" beginning in kindergarten (if not before). Students experience developmentally appropriate comprehension instruction and teaching from their earliest years of schooling, encountering and thinking through information and ideas in a wide variety of texts. Combined with *Toolkit* practices, the sessions in *Scaffolding* zero in on these, as well as other Common Core State Standards for English language arts.

From the Reading Standards for Informational Text K–5:

Standard 1 (grade 3): Ask and answer questions to demonstrate understanding of a text, referring explicitly to the text as the basis for the answers.

Standard 2 (grade 5): Determine two or more main ideas of a text and explain how they are supported by key details; summarize the text.

Standard 6 (grade 3): Distinguish their own point of view from that of the author of a text.

Standard 7 (grade 4): Interpret information presented visually, orally, or quantitatively (e.g., in charts, graphs, diagrams, time lines, animations, or interactive elements on Web pages) and explain how the information contributes to an understanding of the text in which it appears.

From the Speaking and Listening Standards K–5 (grade 5):

Engage effectively in a range of collaborative discussions (one on one, in groups, and teacher-led) with diverse partners *on grade 5 appropriate topics and texts*, building on others' ideas and expressing their own clearly.

To our way of thinking, these standards aren't simply items to check off on an instructional to-do list. *Toolkit* practices create an environment in which thinking routines, comprehension strategies, and content-rich conversations are integral to ongoing, everyday reading instruction. Children are encouraged to become lifelong learners who read actively and independently across the curriculum and who engage their minds and understand what they read. The following sections of this Introduction discuss how this can happen in inclusive, linguistically and culturally diverse classroom settings.

Good Teaching Practices Matter: Building an Inclusive Classroom Community

Whole-group instruction, small-group sessions, and the gradual release of responsibility approach are foundations of *Toolkit* and *Scaffolding* lessons. In *Toolkit* whole-group learning, kids participate in guided discussions designed to get at significant issues, ideas, and concepts. The teacher is more of a "guide on the side" than a "sage on the stage"—so that kids spend much of the lesson interacting with one another as they read, listen, view, talk, draw, and write. Rich talk about text provides students learning English with the sophisticated language and thinking that support their growing understanding and long-term learning. Discussions about shared texts build a community of learners, thinkers, and communicators who ask questions, debate opinions, actively use knowledge, work as a team, and ultimately care about each other and their place in the world.

We emphasize whole-group instruction in the *Toolkits* because we want all kids—no matter what their language background—to engage in spirited discussions and interactions about their reading. Children, regardless of their level of English proficiency, learn a great deal from their peers as they listen to the ongoing discussion and contribute their ideas to these whole-class conversations. All kids should experience a language environment that surrounds them with thoughtful conversations about texts and content. The last thing kids who may require additional language or content support need is to be pulled out during a language- and concept-rich whole-class *Toolkit* lesson.

That's why the small-group Preview sessions in this resource provide English learners with an advance "snapshot" of what will happen during whole-group *Toolkit* instruction so they are fully prepared to participate actively in the lesson. The gradual release of responsibility framework provides the structure for these Preview sessions—teacher modeling that is short and sweet combined with guided practice that introduces kids to content vocabulary and concepts and let's them practice thinking strategies in a small, interactive group setting. As in the whole-group *Toolkit* lesson, children sit together so they can interact with each other, and the teacher can listen in and observe how well they are understanding what is going on. Kids turn, talk, and collaborate to make meaning. An interactive discussion allows the teacher to see what students are thinking and learning, so that he or she can adjust instruction to meet individual needs.

During the whole-group *Toolkit* lesson, the teacher checks in with English learners as she confers with students during guided practice. She may reinforce a vocabulary word or concept with kids who need a bit of reteaching or support children to continue and extend the written responses they began during the small-group preview before the lesson. Making sure kids have a solid understanding of the focus comprehension strategy prepares them to work on their own or in pairs during independent practice. Ongoing assessment and observations allow the teacher to make mid-lesson corrections and plan subsequent instruction for both native and second language speakers. All of these practices allow teachers to differentiate instruction and teach responsively.

This process of moving from modeling, to guided practice, to collaborative and independent practice falls under the instructional approach known as the *gradual release of responsibility*. (See *The Primary Comprehension Toolkit* Teacher's Guide, pages 23 and 24, for more information on gradual release of responsibility.) Gradual release of responsibility is a highly effective teaching model for all learners and is especially so for English language learners. The carefully controlled pacing, extensive opportunities for teacher monitoring, and high degree of teacher and peer support before students are let loose on their own provide optimum scaffolds for both language and comprehension growth.

A User's Guide to This Resource

While the *Toolkit* lessons encourage 24/7 differentiation and work well in classrooms with students who demonstrate a wide range of reading, speaking, and writing proficiencies, this book is intended to help classroom teachers, literacy specialists, ELL specialists, and anyone who works with children learning English enrich and ensure access to the learning environment created through the *Toolkit*.

For every lesson in the *Toolkit*, there is a matching lesson in *Scaffolding The Primary Comprehension Toolkit for English Language Learners*, and each *Scaffolding* lesson contains three main parts, or sessions, that are designed to make learning visible, concrete, and engaging:

1. **Preview the *Toolkit* Lesson** is taught prior to the whole-group *Toolkit* lesson to prepare new speakers of English to actively participate in it. The small-group Preview focuses on content information and comprehension strategies and is designed to last 20–30 minutes

2. **Teach the *Toolkit* Lesson** suggests ways to engage ELLs in the lesson taught from the *Toolkit* strategy book.

3. **Extend the *Toolkit* Lesson** includes two different sessions, both designed to follow the whole-group *Toolkit* lesson:
   - **Language Practice.** This session makes explicit particular aspects of the English language and is usually related to the whole-group lesson, although it can be taught independently of the *Toolkit* lesson.
   - **Content and Comprehension Extensions.** This session both reinforces and extends the learning from the whole-group lessons. Ideally, these learning opportunities are offered to native and second language speakers alike and provide a way to continue the collaborative work begun during the whole-group *Toolkit* lesson.

Before the Toolkit *Lesson*

Preview the *Toolkit* Lesson
- Content, comprehension, and language goals
- Key vocabulary
- Language structures

↓

Teach the *Toolkit* Lesson

↓

After the Toolkit *Lesson*

Extend the *Toolkit* Lesson
- Language Practice
- Content and Comprehension Extensions

The Lesson

Overview Page

Each *Scaffolding* lesson begins with an overview page that lists the content, comprehension, and language goals of the Preview session and highlights the content and comprehension vocabulary as well as the language structures important to understanding and participating in the *Toolkit* lesson. This page notes the teaching content to focus on during the Preview and to keep in mind during the *Toolkit* lesson.

Preview Goals

Giving kids a head start with **content** information, **comprehension** strategies and processes, and specific **language** structures for articulating thinking contributes to making the whole-class *Toolkit* lesson comprehensible for children learning English. During the Preview, we zero in on the content, preparing students to understand the vocabulary and concepts they will need to grasp the ideas and information presented during the lesson.

On the overview page, we list the thinking and comprehension strategies we want to review or pre-teach before the *Toolkit* lesson. We highlight the language of comprehension so that students can link the thinking strategies—such as making connections, asking questions, and drawing inferences—to the language they will use to express their thinking in English. Being clear about how to express themselves as they talk about both content information and thinking strategies enables students to become confident participants, especially when they work independently during collaborative and independent practice.

Key Vocabulary

We make a distinction between **comprehension** process vocabulary and **content**-specific vocabulary. Both are listed here; both are essential. Kids need to be able to talk about both their thinking strategies *and* the content they are learning. In the Preview, we introduce comprehension strategies that are integral to the whole-group lesson, teaching the words and language frames kids will use to talk and write about their thinking processes. Content-specific vocabulary is reinforced through conversations and the use of visuals. We build lesson vocabulary and concepts in the Preview by doing picture walks with the text, illustrations, and photographs; by making word walls with text and images; by bringing in real objects for children to explore; by streaming video and exploring interactive websites; and by role-playing or acting out different scenarios. Visuals and anchor charts that make the vocabulary, information, and comprehension strategies explicit are co-created by teachers and kids and used later to support kids' participation in the *Toolkit* lesson.

Language Structures

We use a variety of language structures or language frames as a linguistic scaffold or bridge that supports students to express their new learning and acquire academic language. The language frames and structures we introduce in the Preview and list here on the overview page link the comprehension and thinking strategies with the language students use to articulate their learning and understanding. The language structures support our introduction of the comprehension strategies and instructional routines that are the focus of the whole-group lesson. Creating a consistent and common language across the grades saves kids from having to figure out and contend with ever-changing instructional jargon. In the Preview, we familiarize students with the language frames and structures that allow them to articulate and share their thinking so that they begin to internalize the comprehension strategies as tools for learning.

Work on these language structures during the Preview provides kids with a starting point for discussion and scaffolds instruction so that when kids participate in the lesson, we know they have a better shot at understanding what is going on. The question "How do you say that?" is answered. Using these structures and frames, the teacher and students explicitly talk about their thinking, draw or sketch their ideas and thoughts, and respond both to the text and to each other. Introducing specific language structures provides students the opportunity to express themselves through discussion and writing and supports the way we talk and write in an academic setting.

The Lesson *(continued)*

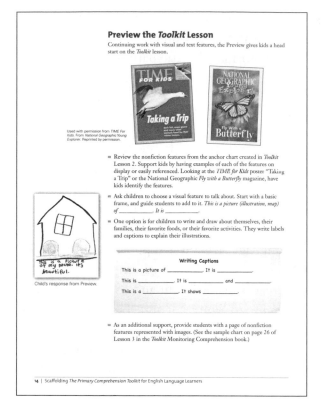

Preview the *Toolkit* Lesson

We begin the Preview by setting clear purposes, focusing on content, comprehension, and language goals. Next, we address content- and comprehension-specific vocabulary used in the *Toolkit* lesson. Finally, we link the comprehension strategy or strategies being taught with the specific language structures, or frames, students will use during the *Toolkit* lesson.

The purpose of the Preview is to make sure students are ready to engage with the content and comprehension strategies central to the whole-group lesson. During the Preview, we:

- introduce key concepts, vocabulary, and ideas important to lesson content.

- pre-teach comprehension and thinking strategies that are the focus of the lesson.

- use photographs, illustrations, and real objects to make content vocabulary and concepts in the text comprehensible.

- create and use images to make thinking visible and support students' comprehension of the text they will be reading and writing.

- introduce and practice language structures children use to talk about content and articulate the thinking strategies that are the focus of the lesson.

- build anchor charts for language structures, vocabulary, and content that support students during the whole-group lesson.

- practice instructional routines that encourage students to express themselves as a way of advancing participation during the whole-group lesson. This supports children as they move toward independence during the practice portions of the *Toolkit* lesson.

The Preview builds students' confidence and provides them an opportunity to practice particular aspects of the lesson that may be challenging for new speakers of English. They do this as part of a supportive group with explicit teacher guidance and extensive conversation. These sessions allow the children abundant think time as well as the chance to talk about their ideas and questions while providing a space to lessen the anxiety that may come when speaking a new language.

During the Preview, it is important to encourage and celebrate students' language approximations. "Give it a try!" is the rallying cry when the teacher can give the students the attention needed to work on content vocabulary and comprehension goals. Teachers have the opportunity to quickly assess where kids are with respect to understanding the content and comprehension strategies. Time spent on a good Preview lesson gives the kids a solid understanding of what will happen in the *Toolkit* lesson and ensures that the information is more comprehensible and that there are fewer surprises.

The Lesson *(continued)*

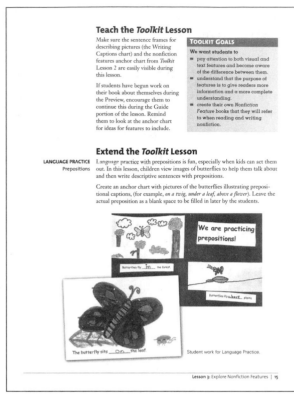

Teach the *Toolkit* Lesson

Make sure the sentence frames for describing pictures (the Writing Captions chart) and the nonfiction features anchor chart from *Toolkit* Lesson 2 are easily visible during this lesson.

If students have begun work on their book about themselves during the Preview, encourage them to continue this during the Guide portion of the lesson. Remind them to look at the anchor chart for ideas for features to include.

TOOLKIT GOALS

We want students to
- pay attention to both visual and text features and become aware of the difference between them.
- understand that the purpose of features is to give readers more information and a more complete understanding.
- create their own *Nonfiction Feature* books that they will refer to when reading and writing nonfiction.

Extend the *Toolkit* Lesson

LANGUAGE PRACTICE **Prepositions**

Language practice with prepositions is fun, especially when kids can act them out. In this lesson, children view images of butterflies to help them talk about and then write descriptive sentences with prepositions.

Create an anchor chart with pictures of the butterflies illustrating prepositional captions, (for example, *on a twig, under a leaf, above a flower*). Leave the actual preposition as a blank space to be filled in later by the students.

Student work for Language Practice.

Lesson 3: Explore Nonfiction Features | 15

Teach the *Toolkit* Lesson

As we teach the whole-group *Toolkit* lesson, we use the anchor charts, language frames, and any other visuals we developed with the students during the Preview. These scaffolds support English language learners, reminding them of the content vocabulary as well as the language and thinking strategies they will use during the lesson. Each lesson, of course, follows the gradual release of responsibility framework, which is the cornerstone of classroom instruction that supports all children as learners but is especially important as we teach children learning English. As we teach the *Toolkit* lesson, we keep in mind the following for our English language learners:

- Children learning English often have a great deal of background knowledge about the lesson content or topic; they may simply not be able to express it in English. When kids have already accessed and discussed their background knowledge (regardless of whether they have done this in their home language and/or English), they will be more prepared to and confident about sharing what they already know during the large-group lesson.

- We invite children who have participated in the Preview to occasionally teach the whole class some of what they have learned during the Preview. This gives their learning from the Preview a clear purpose and encourages all kids to activate and discuss their background knowledge about the topic.

- During modeling and guided practice, kids are encouraged to turn and talk in a language they choose and then try to express their ideas in English. Talking and conversing in any language solidify conceptual understanding.

- During modeling, kids turn and talk frequently so that they stay engaged and, through their conversations, process what the teacher is doing and saying. Turning and talking to share thinking is extremely important for English learners so that they can rehearse comments and thinking they would like to share out with the whole group. When kids try out their ideas with a partner first, they are more confident and they worry less about making a mistake.

- As children participate in the discussion, teachers have an opportunity to mediate and support children to expand on their responses. We encourage all kids to extend their responses by saying: "Tell me more about what you are thinking." "Can you say more?" "What else do you think?" This added support is particularly important for English learners, and when we model this "Tell me more" language, kids often use these same encouraging comments with their classmates.

- Guided practice is an important part of the whole-group lesson. It enables students to work collaboratively before they are asked to work independently. Students can practice what is expected of them with a partner, and this provides students who may need more help with opportunities to take a risk with plenty of peer support.

- Guided practice also gives the teacher the opportunity to quickly check that students understand what they are being asked to do and correct any misunderstandings.

- As kids move into collaborative and independent practice, we make note if some children need to review a concept or strategy and spontaneously gather a small group for a quick recap. Students can opt to remain on the rug for a quick review if they would like more guidance before going off on their own. This extra attention can make the difference between a confused and a confident independent learner.

- Conferences during independent and collaborative practice enable us to tailor instruction to children's individual needs, including second language needs. We might briefly reteach a vocabulary word or concept that children may not have grasped initially. We continue to model language that students can use as they continue to work with each other during collaborative practice.

- During collaborative and independent practice, we ask children to rehearse what they plan to share with the entire group. This gives all kids more confidence to take a risk speaking in front of the class and is especially helpful for children presenting in a second language. As we confer, we encourage students to organize their thoughts, suggesting, "You should say that when we share! Say it again so I remember what you said."

The Lesson (continued)

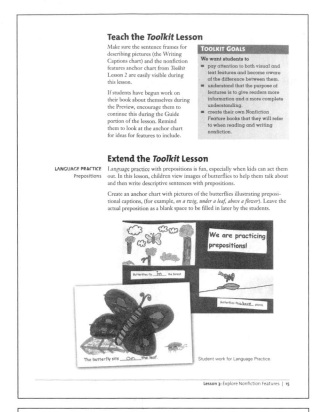

Teach the *Toolkit* Lesson

Make sure the sentence frames for describing pictures (the Writing Captions chart) and the nonfiction features anchor chart from *Toolkit* Lesson 2 are easily visible during this lesson.

If students have begun work on their book about themselves during the Preview, encourage them to continue this during the Guide portion of the lesson. Remind them to look at the anchor chart for ideas for features to include.

TOOLKIT GOALS

We want students to

- pay attention to both visual and text features and become aware of the difference between them.
- understand that the purpose of features is to give readers more information and a more complete understanding.
- create their own *Nonfiction Feature* books that they will refer to when reading and writing nonfiction.

Extend the *Toolkit* Lesson

LANGUAGE PRACTICE Prepositions

Language practice with prepositions is fun, especially when kids can act them out. In this lesson, children view images of butterflies to help them talk about and then write descriptive sentences with prepositions.

Create an anchor chart with pictures of the butterflies illustrating prepositional captions, (for example, *on a twig, under a leaf, above a flower*). Leave the actual preposition as a blank space to be filled in later by the students.

Student work for Language Practice.

Lesson 3: Explore Nonfiction Features | 15

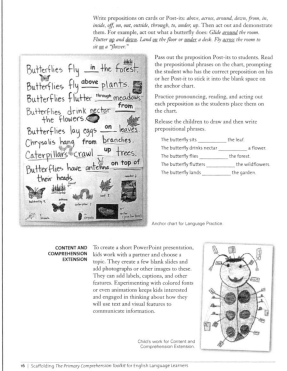

Write prepositions on cards or Post-its: *above, across, around, down, from, in, inside, off, on, out, outside, through, to, under, up*. Then act out and demonstrate them. For example, act out what a butterfly does: *Glide around the room. Flutter up and down. Land on the floor or under a desk. Fly across the room to sit on a "flower."*

Pass out the preposition Post-its to students. Read the prepositional phrases on the chart, prompting the student who has the correct preposition on his or her Post-it to stick it into the blank space on the anchor chart.

Practice pronouncing, reading, and acting out each preposition as the students place them on the chart.

Release the children to draw and then write prepositional phrases.

The butterfly sits _____ the leaf.
The butterfly drinks nectar _____ a flower.
The butterfly flies _____ the forest.
The butterfly flutters _____ the wildflowers.
The butterfly lands _____ the garden.

Anchor chart for Language Practice.

CONTENT AND COMPREHENSION EXTENSION

To create a short PowerPoint presentation, kids work with a partner and choose a topic. They create a few blank slides and add photographs or other images to these. They can add labels, captions, and other features. Experimenting with colored fonts or even animations keeps kids interested and engaged in thinking about how they will use text and visual features to communicate information.

Child's work for Content and Comprehension Extension.

16 | Scaffolding *The Primary Comprehension Toolkit* for English Language Learners

Extend the *Toolkit* Lesson

After the whole-group *Toolkit* lesson, we convene small-group sessions to reinforce and extend the work that was begun during the lesson.

Language Practice

Language practice sessions provide explicit practice with grammar, syntax, and oracy and, in most cases, are related to lesson content. *Oracy* is defined as those aspects of oral language that need to be explicitly taught and practiced by students learning English. Explicit practice with more abstract grammatical structures, idioms, modal verbs, conditional phrases, and other aspects of language is important to children's developing knowledge of a new language. The focused language practice in these sessions supports children studying a new language to more easily articulate their thinking and become more confident speakers and writers. The lessons are designed so that children at a variety of language stages can access them and teachers can easily differentiate to meet the needs of the students.

Content and Comprehension Extensions

To build a strong foundation for thinking, learning, and understanding in the disciplines of literature, science, and social studies, kids need exposure to many topics, ideas, and issues as well as the time to delve into them. Although the *Toolkit* lessons cover many different topics, these sessions are an opportunity go a little deeper and extend children's learning to develop their vocabulary and content knowledge as fully as possible. Many of the extensions emphasize active learning with online sources or collaborative projects that take thinking further.

Options for extensions provide the whole class and/or English language learners with opportunities to engage in higher-level thinking tasks as they pursue some aspect of the lesson topic that interests them. The extensions also encourage kids to apply the comprehension strategies learned during the lesson to other contexts and tasks. We specifically design ways in which kids can create in-depth projects and investigate their own questions.

The sessions that surround the *Toolkit* lesson—the Preview, Language Practice, and Content and Comprehension Extensions—encourage collaboration around *Toolkit* comprehension instruction, all day and every day. These practices, we believe, give children learning a new language the best chance to become thoughtful comprehenders and increasingly independent readers, writers, and thinkers.

The Content and Comprehension Extensions are appropriate for small groups or the whole class. They provide time for students to delve more deeply into topics and questions prompted by the *Toolkit* lesson. All children benefit from participating in discussions, investigations, and projects in a linguistically diverse group that encourages kids to pursue their own interests and questions. While these sessions are teacher-guided initially to launch kids into extended study, they are designed to encourage pairs or small groups of children to continue the work on their own, without the direct involvement of the teacher.

How to Use This Resource

In culturally and linguistically diverse schools, literacy instruction for both native speakers of English and for children learning English takes many forms and configurations. This resource is designed for maximum flexibility so that classroom teachers and ELL specialists can design instruction that best fits their school's model. Regardless of programs or instructional models, the most effective collaborative efforts involve all the teachers in a building: classroom teachers, ELL specialists, librarians, special ed teachers, literacy specialists, and anyone else for that matter. Collaborative instruction is a powerful force that energizes everyone to be responsible for all students' learning and to continually refine and improve their teaching practices. When teachers plan together, teach together, and meet together to reflect on kids' learning, this has a real and lasting effect on the quality of instruction.

Classroom Configurations and Instructional Options

The lessons in *Scaffolding* The Primary Comprehension Toolkit *for English Language Learners* can be used as teachers work together in classrooms in which:

- all or most of the students are native English speakers with a small group of English learners who speak a variety of different home, or heritage, languages.

- all or most of the students are native English speakers with a small group of English learners, most of whom speak the same home language.

- all or most of the children are learning English and may speak many different languages.

- all or most of the children are learning English, and many or all have a home language in common.

On the two following pages, we have outlined a variety of teaching options for classrooms with students of differing language backgrounds. While the optimum situation is one in which classroom teachers and ESL specialists collaborate on teaching the Preview, Language Practice, and Content and Comprehension Extensions sessions, all sessions are short enough to be taught by the classroom teacher.

Class Composition and Teaching Options

Class Composition	Teaching Options	How Can I Organize and Manage This?
Primarily native English speakers and some ELLs with varying language backgrounds	**Classroom teacher** The classroom teacher does the Preview and Language Practice with a small groups of ELLs.	Preview and Language Practice sessions are short and focused—the teacher convenes the small group while other children work on their own, reading, writing, participating in centers, doing research, etc.
	Classroom teacher collaborates with ESL specialist An ESL specialist who works with small groups in the classroom during the literacy block teaches the Preview before the *Toolkit* lesson and Language Practice session after it. If possible, he or she works with the whole class, including ELLs, during the *Toolkit* lesson.	Collaboration between the classroom teacher and ESL specialist is encouraged. Sharing the responsibility for teaching the sessions and *Toolkit* lessons and working as a team are the best way to meet the individual needs of all kids.
Primarily native English speakers and some ELLs from the same language background	**Classroom teacher** The classroom teacher does the Preview and Language Practice with a group of ELLs. The rest of the class works independently during these small-group sessions. (See several suggestions for managing independent work time below.)	Children turn and talk in their home language even if the teacher does not speak it. This can build children's confidence so they participate as the lesson continues in English. If the teacher speaks the children's home language, this can be worked into the Preview to provide more support for transitioning from one language to another.
	Classroom teacher collaborates with ESL teacher or another teacher who can support children's home language If the teacher or another adult in the classroom speaks the children's native language, using it during the Preview can support children to use both languages.	The classroom teacher and ESL teacher co-teach lessons and plan together how to best merge the Preview and Language Practice sessions with *Toolkit* instruction. The idea is to maintain cohesiveness among the different parts of the lesson so that students are better able to understand the content and participate.

Class Composition	Teaching Options	How Can I Organize and Manage This?
All or most of the class are ELLs who speak a common language or are from varying language backgrounds (continued)	**Classroom teacher** The classroom teacher teaches the Preview with the whole class. The Preview is adapted to language needs of the students.	The Preview can be used flexibly so that it makes sense for all children to participate in it.
	Classroom teacher collaborates with ESL specialist With support from an ESL teacher, the two teachers can do the Preview together. If the ESL teacher works in the classroom, the Preview can be more carefully targeted to the language needs of the children. For instance, one teacher might work with newer speakers of English who need a more extensive preview. If the ESL teacher works with ELLs outside the classroom, providing a solid Preview experience as well as Language Practice and Extension sessions, close collaboration between the classroom teacher and ESL teacher is necessary for coherent and well-thought-out instruction both inside and outside the classroom.	The classroom teacher and ESL teacher co-teach lessons and work and plan together how to best merge the Preview and Language Practice sessions with *Toolkit* instruction. The idea is to maintain cohesiveness among the different parts of the lesson so that students are better able to understand the content and participate.
Bilingual/dual language classrooms	**Classroom teacher** The *Toolkit* lessons can be taught as is, in English, with the Preview, Language Practice, and Content and Comprehension Extensions we recommend, or a bilingual teacher can deliver the *Toolkit* lesson in the children's home language and do the Language Practice as an English language development lesson.	Planning for bilingual instruction may take more time and preparation because it involves finding available materials in other languages. (See *Toolkit Texts* for articles at different reading levels that are in both English and Spanish.)
	Team teaching This is particularly effective with teachers of both English and Spanish (or whatever other common language students share) or a classroom teacher with an ESL specialist. Of course, instruction is most effective when teachers plan and focus their instruction on students' specific language and learning needs.	This option gives the students a knowledge base in their heritage language that they can transfer to English. The Language Practice sessions provide English learners with explicit grammar and oracy practice in their new language.

Pacing Considerations

Many teachers teach a whole-group *Toolkit* lesson once or twice a week, and then on the days following each lesson, children practice these same *Toolkit* strategies in their own reading. Children learning English, of course, also need plenty of time to practice using the *Toolkit* strategies as they read independently. But this is also a time when a small group can meet for a short time to focus on the Language Practice related to a particular lesson. Again, in collaboration with an ESL specialist, either the classroom teacher or the specialist can work with the small group while the other teacher confers with students who are working on their own.

Content and Comprehension Extensions can take place almost anytime kids are able to work on their own—especially during reader's and writer's workshop. There are additional suggestions for taking *Toolkit* instruction into content areas such as science and social studies in *The Primary Toolkit* Teacher's Guide, pages 59–64.

Pacing Possibilities

Day 1	Day 2	Day 3	Day 4
Convene a small group and teach the **Preview** for the upcoming *Toolkit* lesson while the whole class works independently.	Teach the **whole-group** *Toolkit* **lesson**. Complete the modeling and guided practice portions of the lessons. Begin collaborative and independent practice with the whole group.	The class continues to engage in collaborative and independent practice with the *Toolkit* focus strategy from Day 2.	Children continue practicing the strategy in their own reading.
If an ESL specialist is available, the ESL teacher teaches the **Preview** as the rest of the students work on their own. The classroom teacher can move around the room conferring with individuals or pairs of students or can convene other flexible small groups based on needs.	With an ESL specialist present, both the classroom teacher and ESL specialist can confer with individuals and pairs, identifying students who might benefit from the follow-up **Language Practice** session. An option is to teach this following the *Toolkit* lesson or on Day 3.	Provide a **Language Practice** session for English learners during this time, taught by either the ESL specialist or the classroom teacher. Begin a **Content and Comprehension Extension** for a small or large group.	Extend the **Content and Comprehension Extension** session for interested kids or the whole class, including native English speakers as well as English learners. Kids use *Toolkit* practices and strategies to pursue their own research and projects.

Small-Group Instruction

Children differ, and the most effective use of this resource occurs when we convene a group of kids who will find the whole-group lesson much more comprehensible because they have experienced the small-group Preview and Extension sessions. Participating in the Language Practice and Content and Comprehension Extension sessions reinforces and extends the language and grammatical structures and the content concepts and ideas from the *Toolkit* lesson. With the ESL specialist or other support staff, decide which children would benefit from the Preview, Language Practice, and Content and Comprehension Extensions. The goal of this resource is to target carefully scaffolded instruction to the language and comprehension needs of kids. Children participating in these different sessions may or may not be the same group of children.

When convening a small group, consider:

- how accessible the content is for English learners. Convene a group of children who are unfamiliar with the specific vocabulary or concepts surrounding the lesson. Prepare the suggested anchor charts or visuals ahead of time so that maximum instructional time can be spent interacting with the students.

- the children's familiarity with a particular comprehension strategy or strategies. If you know that the comprehension language and strategy are new to some students, emphasize the thinking strategies and language structures in the Preview.

- the children's proficiency with grammar and oracy, particularly related to the content of specific Language Practice sessions.

- finding a time in the day when most of the class is working independently to allow you 20–30 minutes with a small group. Most schools with children learning English set aside time for ELL instruction—either by the classroom teacher or by a specialist. Teaching the Preview and/or Language Practice sessions is an excellent use of instructional time designated for English learners. If you are working with a reading specialist or language specialist, make the Preview, Language Practice, and Content and Comprehension Extensions sessions an instructional priority for one of you. Teaching the Preview the day before the whole-group *Toolkit* lesson works well. Or, teaching it on the same day, right before the *Toolkit* lesson, ensures that the new information and ideas are fresh in the kids' minds for the whole-group lesson.

Creating and managing small groups require time and effort from both teaching teams and the solo classroom teacher—but the differentiated instruction that small-group teaching fosters has clear benefits for the individual learner. Still, the question most often asked is: *What are the other kids doing while I teach small groups?* When we meet with small groups, the rest of the class is engaged in reading, writing, and researching. To make sure kids experience meaningful collaborative and independent practice, the following instructional and management strategies have proved helpful. A classroom environment that encourages independent learning includes:

- small tables, work stations, or centers with easily accessible books, photographs, and other resources that kids can and want to read.

- easily accessible and copious supplies such as markers, pens, pencils, different-sized paper, posterboard, and stapled pages for blank books to encourage kids to respond to learning.

- easily viewed posters and anchor charts from previous *Toolkit* lessons that guide kids as they read, write, and respond using a variety of comprehension strategies.

- access to a potpourri of familiar thinksheets and scaffolds so kids can record their thinking on their own or with a partner.

- response journals, content notebooks, and other ongoing response options so that kids can keep track of their learning and thinking as they read, write, talk, draw, and investigate.

Following are some examples of collaborative tasks, centers, and work spaces that are engaging for kids.

Nonfiction Feature Center. Kids choose from magazines, photographs, books, approved websites, and other resources that are engaging and accessible. They read, view, and write about the information, creating their own page or poster using appropriate nonfiction features to organize and share their new learning. Posting the Nonfiction Feature Chart created during *Toolkit* lessons guides kids to incorporate a variety of features as they write to teach others what they have learned. This center can be created after the Monitor Comprehension and Activate & Connect lessons.

Make Connections with Realistic Fiction. Following Lesson 6, put together a text set of realistic fiction picture books that kids can really connect to—making text-to-self, text-to-text, and text-to-world connections. Kids use thinksheets like the Connection/How it helped me understand scaffold to monitor and reflect on their understanding.

Research Center: Investigate on Your Own! At this center, kids use a variety of think sheets and note-taking scaffolds to find out more about current classroom science or social studies topics. Resources can include books, visuals, CDs, interactive website links or recommendations, and other resources that will extend kids' knowledge about a topic under study. Favorite note-taking scaffolds include:

- Notes/Thinking
- What I Learned/ What I Wonder/ Wow!
- Facts/Questions/ Responses

The Content and Comprehension Extensions with each lesson in this resource have ideas for encouraging kids to investigate and explore on their own.

Book Conversations. What does Smokey Daniels suggest kids do after they finish reading a book? Talk about it with someone and then choose another book to read! "Keep On Reading" might be a *Toolkit* mantra, but we know that kids don't always fully understand thinking and comprehension strategies after one or two group lessons. What better way to provide meaningful work and reinforce *Toolkit* instruction than to set up a conversation corner (or center) where kids can talk about what they read? Several suggestions recommended in *The Daily Five* (Boushey and Moser 2006) might be helpful:

- Kids read (and talk) to someone about their reading.
- Kids (talk and) write about their reading.
- Kids listen to a friend talk about his or her great read.

For ideas for more extensive literature circles and even inquiry circles where kids work together to investigate a topic they are curious about, see *Comprehension and Collaboration* (Harvey and Daniels 2009).

Collaboration Is Key

Rather than developing or implementing several different programs for linguistically diverse students as well as those children who are native speakers of English, we believe it is essential to create one instructional plan that is responsive to the learning and language needs of all the kids in the school (Commins and Miramontes 2005). But this requires that classroom teachers and specialists make a deliberate and sustained effort to collaborate. When teachers and the principal collaborate on instruction together on a regular basis, the result is an inclusive and cohesive plan that translates into consistent instruction within and across grade levels. The time spent planning content lessons and differentiated reading, writing, and language instruction supports all kids, not just children learning English, to access and understand the content and the curriculum.

Before you teach a specific set of *Toolkit* strategy lessons, it is helpful for classroom teachers and the appropriate specialists to plan together and create a vision for *Toolkit* instruction with English language learners, including pacing, timing, and differentiated instruction. It takes a village to meet the needs of linguistically and culturally diverse students, and making sure the adults in the environment all understand their responsibilities and roles will go a long way in ensuring successful implementation.

See *The Primary Comprehension Toolkit* Teacher's Guide, pages 50–55, for ways that *Toolkit* instruction can be planned to fit into the school day and year.

Emphasizing *Toolkit* Principles and Practices with Culturally and Linguistically Diverse Students

The following foundational principles and practices found throughout *The Comprehension Toolkits* are particularly important as we teach linguistically and culturally diverse students. When teachers put these practices to work in classrooms, they create powerful opportunities for teaching and learning with children who are learning English as a new language. For additional information on each of these areas, consult the *Toolkit* Teacher's Guides.

Immerse kids in nonfiction.

If it's important for all kids to become immersed in nonfiction, it is essential for children learning English to spend a lot of time reading it. Hands down, it's the most accessible genre for children learning a new language. For more on this, see *The Primary Comprehension Toolkit* Teacher's Guide, pages 8–11.

Make thinking visible.

Multimodal forms of teaching and learning heighten children's engagement throughout our sessions for English learners and the whole-group *Toolkit* lessons. Posters, anchor charts, features, and many visuals make the written and spoken words more comprehensible for children learning a new language. Meaning is made explicit when kids view, touch, feel, experience, listen, read, write, talk, draw, and dramatize. In short, they experience and then create and construct the language, actions, and ideas that further their knowledge of the world.

Making our words and thinking visible and as concrete as possible means that teachers and kids co-construct many different kinds of anchor charts to display throughout the room during the lessons. We model for kids how to represent their thinking with a quick sketch or drawing or with a scenario they dramatize. Working in different modalities helps kids show what they know or think and provides helpful scaffolds as they talk about and share their learning. For more on making thinking visible, see *The Primary Comprehension Toolkit* Teacher's Guide, pages 27 and 28.

Teach a common language for learning.

Creating a common language for literacy and learning builds a foundation for students to work from in both the acquisition of English and the comprehensive use of academic language. For kids learning a new language, having a clear, consistent language that describes thinking and learning routines is essential.

Our definition of a common language includes specific strategy language as well as language that guides thinking routines and social/academic interactions. See *The Primary Comprehension Toolkit* Teacher's Guide, page 17.

Activate and build background knowledge.

An essential *Toolkit* principle is that reading is all about kids constructing their own knowledge. The more kids learn, the more background knowledge they bring to their learning, which in turn fosters further learning! If children find it difficult to share their background knowledge in English, we suggest they share this knowledge in their home language or activate it through drawing or dramatizing what they already know and understand. We take careful notice of what they already know and understand, and we go from there. See *The Primary Comprehension Toolkit*, page 18, for suggestions for building kids' knowledge around real-world reading.

Create flexible small groups.

Collaborative conversations take place in breakout spaces and areas around the room designed to encourage teacher-student and student-student inter-actions. We co-construct meaning in large groups, small groups, conferences, and discussions so that student talk happens all day long. For children learning English, this process begins during the Preview and naturally continues in the whole-group lesson. During the Language Practice session, teachers can target the specific language needs of a small group of students who may need grammar or oracy practice. Working in small, needs-based flexible groups provides the perfect complement to whole-group instruction. For more on small groups using the *Toolkit*, see *The Primary Comprehension Toolkit*, pages 25 and 26.

Encourage purposeful talk and conversation.

The *Toolkit* lessons are designed to get students talking! This is especially important for culturally and linguistically diverse students because it gives them the opportunity to interact with their peers. Remember that it is also important to pair children up appropriately with other children who will both support them and challenge them in their learning. Getting kids to talk and discuss in a give-and-take manner is the goal. A give-and-take discussion allows students language practice involving content and builds conceptual understandings. [For more on purposeful talk, see *The Primary Comprehension Toolkit* Teacher's Guide, pages 25 and 26.

Incorporate a wide variety of meaningful texts and visuals.

We think about how best to use print as we teach with visuals and images, anchor charts, enlarged texts and big books, being aware that engagement with all kinds of texts helps build students' comprehension. And if this is true for native English speakers, it is even more so for children learning English. If it can be labeled, label it! If it can be described, describe it! Add sketches to text or use arrows to connect thinking—the more visual images, the better. When students are steeped in meaningful print, they can use that print in their own reading and writing. See *The Primary Comprehension Toolkit* Teacher's Guide, page 16, for more on choosing and using engaging texts.

Scaffold with explicit instruction.

We are as precise and explicit in our teaching as possible. Being clear about our language and comprehension goals keeps the teaching focused so it is clear to kids how they can respond. It is important to make sure students understand what is going on, so we check frequently for understanding, listening carefully to kids as they turn and talk, engaging in think-pair-share activities, and responding in many different ways. For additional information on explicit instruction, see *The Primary Comprehension Toolkit* Teacher's Guide, page 18.

Scaffold instruction using the gradual release of responsibility framework.

Scaffolding instruction with the gradual release of responsibility framework is integral to *Toolkit* language and lessons, so kids can make sense of what we do and say as we teach. The gradual release framework, to our way of thinking, is the mother of all scaffolds! The notion of scaffolding underlies how we differentiate instruction so as to be responsive to children's various language levels and proficiencies. Each step in the *Toolkit* lesson gradually releases responsibility to students, and we have taken the same approach with these sessions for English learners. Each session—the Preview, the *Toolkit* lesson, the Language Practice, and Content and Comprehension Extensions—is responsive to the learning needs of culturally and linguistically diverse students and continually moves kids toward independence. See *The Primary Comprehension Toolkit* Teacher's Guide, pages 23 and 24, for more information on gradual release of responsibility.

These principles and practices make sense for all kids, and both *Toolkit* and *Scaffolding* lessons embrace them—launching kids into active literacy practices that put children front and center in the instructional process.

References

Allington, Richard. 2009. *What Really Matters in Response to Intervention*. New York: Teachers College Press.

Boushey, Gail, and Joan Moser. 2006. *The Daily Five*. Portland, ME: Stenhouse.

Buhrow, Brad, and Anne Upczak-Garcia. 2006. *Ladybugs, Tornadoes and Swirling Galaxies: English Language Learners Discover Their World Through Inquiry*. Portland, ME: Stenhouse.

Chen, Linda, and Eugenia Mora-Flores. 2006. *Balanced Literacy for English Language Learners*, K–2. Portsmouth, NH: Heinemann.

Commins, Nancy. 2011. "Meaning Is Everything" in *Comprehension Going Forward*. Harvey Daniels, ed. Portsmouth, NH: Heinemann.

Commins, Nancy, and Ofelia Miramontes. 2005. *Linguistic Diversity and Teaching*. Mahwah, NJ: Lawrence Erlbaum Associates, Inc.

Cummins, Jim. 2009. Foreword in *English Learners, Academic Literacy and Thinking* by Pauline Gibbons. Portsmouth, NH: Heinemann.

Echevarria, Janet, MaryEllen Vogt, and Deborah Short. 2000. *Making Content Comprehensible for English Language Learners*. Boston: Allyn & Bacon.

Gentile, Lance. 2004. *The Oracy Instructional Guide*. Carlsbad, CA: Dominie Press, Inc.

Gibbons, Pauline. 2009. *English Learners, Academic Literacy, and Thinking*. Portsmouth, NH: Heinemann.

Gibbons, Pauline. 2002. *Scaffolding Language, Scaffolding Learning: Teaching Second Language Learners in the Mainstream Classroom*. Portsmouth, NH: Heinemann.

Goudvis, Anne, and Stephanie Harvey. 2005. *Reading the World: Content Comprehension with Linguistically Diverse Learners* (video). Portland, ME: Stenhouse.

Harvey, Stephanie, and Harvey Daniels. 2009. *Comprehension and Collaboration*. Portsmouth, NH: Heinemann.

Harvey, Stephanie, and Anne Goudvis. 2007. *Strategies That Work*, 2nd. ed. Portland, ME: Stenhouse.

Herrera, Socorro, Della Perez, and Kathy Escamilla. 2009. *Teaching Reading to English Language Learners*. Boston: Allyn & Bacon.

Mohr, Kathleen, and Eric Mohr. 2007. "Extending English-language learners' classroom interactions using the Response Protocol." *The Reading Teacher*, 60(5): 440–450.

National Governors Association Center for Best Practices and Council of Chief State School Officers. 2010. *Common Core State Standards for English Language Arts*.

Thomas, W., and V. Collier. 1999. *School Effectiveness for Language Minority Students*. George Washington University, Washington, DC: National Clearinghouse for Bilingual Education.

Wood, David, Jerome Bruner, and Gail Ross. 1976. "The Role of Tutoring in Problem Solving." *Journal of Psychology and Psychiatry* 17(2): 89–100.

THINK ABOUT The Text

Look, listen, talk, write, and draw to express thinking

PREVIEW GOALS

We want students to

CONTENT — understand concepts central to the story, such as compromise.

COMPREHENSION — distinguish between what the story is about and what it makes us think about.

LANGUAGE — become aware of their thinking as they read or listen to the text.

KEY VOCABULARY

COMPREHENSION WORDS
reminds me of
makes me think about

CONTENT WORDS
artist
draw, drew
art teacher
paint
compromise

LANGUAGE STRUCTURES

The language structures introduced in the Preview help students articulate their thinking about connections to their own experiences.

This reminds me of _____.

This makes me think about _____.

I like _____.

I think _____.

Preview the *Toolkit* Lesson

The Preview focuses on the *Toolkit* lesson text by Tomie dePaola titled *The Art Lesson* and one of its underlying themes, the art of compromise.

■ Share the cover and first few pages of *The Art Lesson*, explaining that it was written by Tomie dePaola, a writer and artist. Ask kids to turn and talk about something they like or love to do using *I like* _____.

■ Share the cover and the first few pages of the book. Using the language of making connections, ask students to turn and talk about what it makes them think about. Prompt them with the question "What does this story remind you of?" or "What does this story make you think of?" Scribe their answers for them, and post them on the anchor chart.

What We Are Thinking

This reminds me of _____.

This makes me think about _____.

I like _____.

I think _____.

■ Introduce students to another new frame that supports them to think about the book, the language structure *I think* _____. Now ask students to draw and write their own thoughts on a Post-it.

Anchor chart of language frames used in the Preview.

- One of the underlying themes in the book is compromise. This concept is introduced to students in the Preview. To do this, teach a simple game of role-playing. Using a conflict the class may be experiencing (arguments over who is not sharing markers, who gets to be line leader, etc.), guide students to act out what it is to compromise. For example, kids could say: "I want the red marker." "No, I do." "You use it now, and then it's my turn." "OK." Practice several scenarios so the children begin to gain an understanding that with conflict often comes compromise.

Teach the *Toolkit* Lesson

Hang anchor charts from the Preview with the language frames for students to use. Encourage them to use *I like* _____. and *I think* _____. during Connect and Engage to turn and talk about *The Art Lesson*.

As you discuss the concept of *compromise* during the lesson, have kids who participated in the Preview talk about their role-playing.

TOOLKIT GOALS

We want students to
- develop an awareness of their thinking as they read, listen, and view.
- understand that their thinking matters when they read.
- leave tracks of their thinking by drawing and writing.
- learn how to turn and talk to a partner about their thinking.

Extend the *Toolkit* Lesson

LANGUAGE PRACTICE
Building Vocabulary

The Art Lesson has some very useful art-related vocabulary that students may or may not be familiar with, and this is an opportunity for them to learn this vocabulary and practice using it.

Prior to this session, build a large picture dictionary. Attach art materials—markers, crayons, colored pencils, watercolors, and more—to the anchor chart, and label each object.

To introduce the large picture dictionary, present the idea that Tommy loves to draw and paint. Have *The Art Lesson* handy, and view the sections where Tommy is drawing and painting.

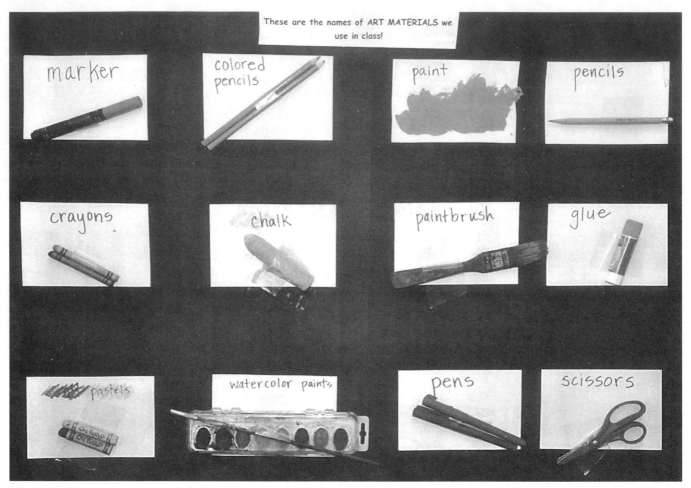

Picture dictionary of art materials for Language Practice.

Ask the children to use the following language frames to practice simple sentences and conditional statements. This will help them to talk about materials in the room and build their vocabulary.

I color with _____.

I paint with _____.

I draw with _____.

I like to draw _____ with _____.

When I _____, I like to use _____.

The students draw images and write with the support of language frames to express the kinds of art supplies they use or like to use.

On the same chart, write the language frame *I chose _____ because _____.*

Then have students share their drawing and writing by talking about the choices they made.

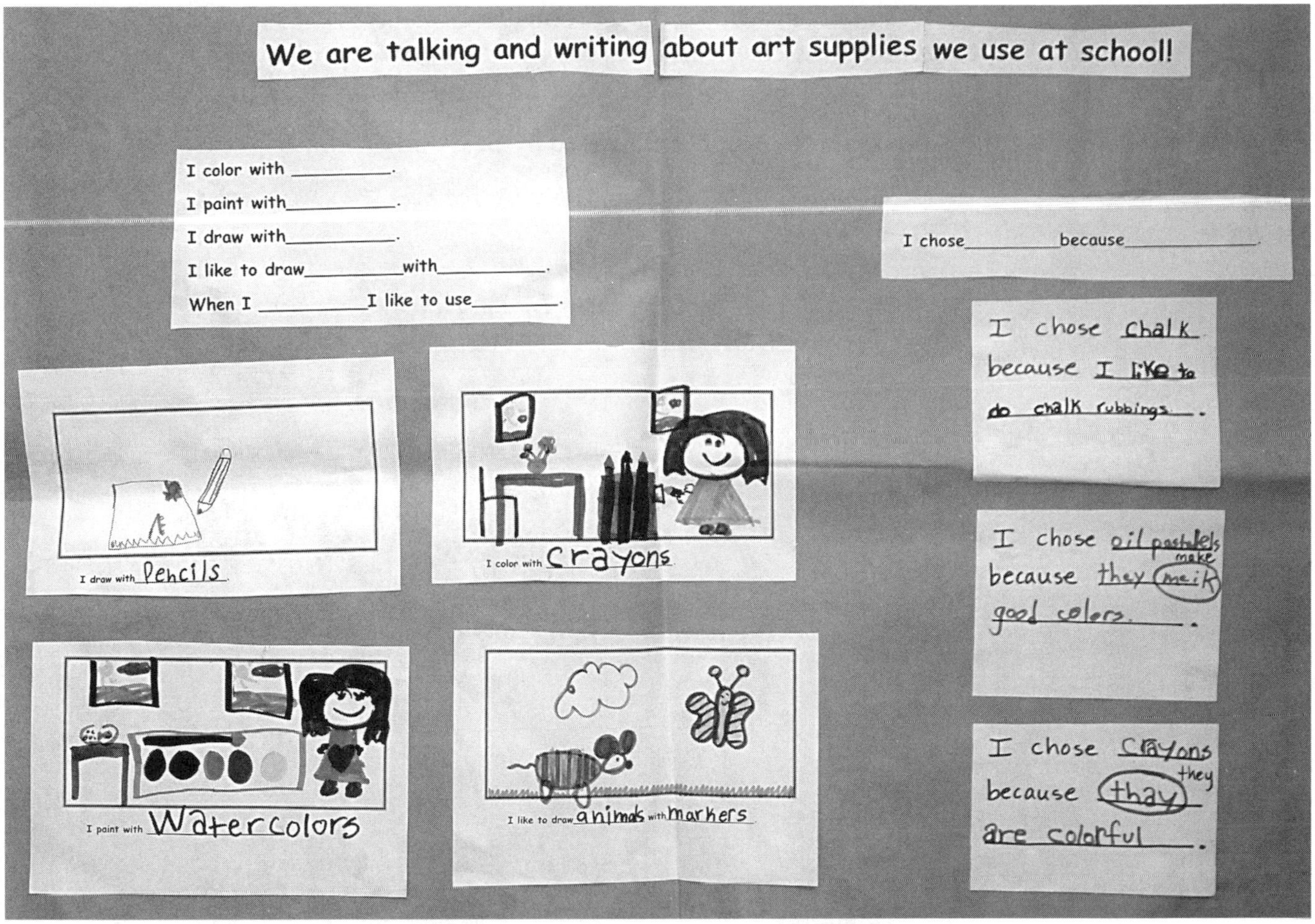

We are talking and writing about art supplies we use at school!

I color with _____.
I paint with_____.
I draw with_____.
I like to draw_____ with_____.
When I _____ I like to use_____.

I chose_____ because_____.

I chose chalk because I like to do chalk rubbings.

I chose oil pastels because they make good colors.

I chose crayons because they are colorful

I draw with Pencils

I color with crayons

I paint with Watercolors

I like to draw animals with markers

Language frames and children's responses for Language Practice.

CONTENT AND COMPREHENSION EXTENSION

A book study of an author and illustrator who uses different artistic methods to communicate his message is a wonderful way to engage students in the world of art and meaning-making through art.

Eric Carle's books are visually appealing and written with poetic yet repetitive language to support developing readers. Read aloud several of his books, noting how Carle uses watercolors to convey imagery. Students may paint a picture based on Carle's illustrations or create versions of Carle's books using other animals. For example, with *Brown Bear, Brown Bear*, kids choose an animal and write about it using the same or a similar language frame:

_____ (color + animal),
_____ (color + animal),
What do you see?

Use a similar language pattern such as *Green snake, green snake, what are you doing?* Answers such as *I am slithering through the grass* give kids practice with high-frequency words and descriptive words. And kids can be creative!

Books written and/or illustrated by Eric Carle include:

> *Brown Bear, Brown Bear, What Do You See?*
> *The Very Busy Caterpillar*
> *The Very Busy Spider*
> *Polar Bear, Polar Bear, What Do You Hear?*
> *The Very Quiet Cricket*

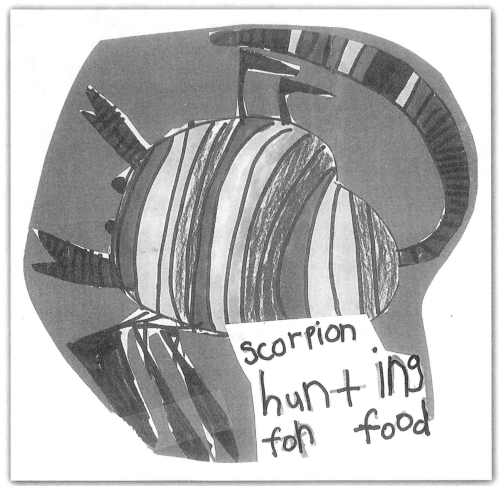

Child's work for Content and Comprehension Extension.

NOTICE and THINK ABOUT Nonfiction Features

Construct a Feature/ Purpose chart

PREVIEW GOALS

We want students to

CONTENT
- notice and use nonfiction features to gather information about a variety of topics.

COMPREHENSION
- express knowledge of a topic using nonfiction features.

LANGUAGE
- identify nonfiction features and their purposes.

KEY VOCABULARY

COMPREHENSION WORDS
features
photographs
captions
illustrations
drawings
maps
labels
table of contents
index
purpose
information

CONTENT WORDS
butterfly
egg
wing
leg
mouth
caterpillar

LANGUAGE STRUCTURES

During the Preview and *Toolkit* lesson, simple phrases help students name the features they notice. Then they practice talking about features and their purposes.

I see _____.
I see a photograph (caption, map, and so on).

I see _____. This feature tells us _____.
I see a photograph. This feature tells us what a butterfly looks like.

Preview the *Toolkit* Lesson

The Preview introduces children to the *Toolkit* lesson text and familiarizes them with the visual and text features that are the focus of Lessons 2 and 3.

From *National Geographic Young Explorer.* Reprinted by permission.

- Ask kids to turn and talk about their background knowledge about butterflies. Have them share out their thinking. Preview butterfly vocabulary.

- Preview the National Geographic magazine titled *Fly with a Butterfly* that will be used during the *Toolkit* lesson. Introduce the word *features* by pointing out specific visual and text features: photograph, label, caption.

- On an anchor chart, post the language frame *I see* _____. Use the *TIME for Kids* poster or another nonfiction text that can be seen in a big version, and point to different features as the kids say "I see a caption" or "I see bold text."

> **Features**
>
> I see _____.
>
> I see _____. This feature tells us _____.

- Guide kids to talk about what the features teach us. Use the language frames *I see* _____. and *I see* _____. *This feature tells us.* Explain that we can talk about the names of features as well as their purposes, what the features teach us. For instance, a photograph shows us exactly what something looks like.

- Explain the word *information*—noting that features can teach us information, or facts, about something. For example, we learn about the butterfly by studying its body parts in the photograph.

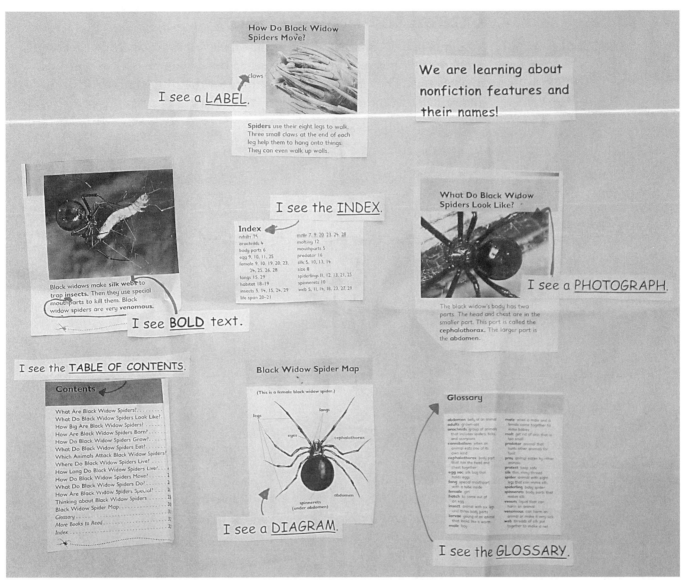

Anchor chart for the Preview.

Teach the *Toolkit* Lesson

Post the language frame chart from the Preview so students can refer to it during the lesson. As you build the chart of features and their purposes, add images and examples of the features to the chart.

To support students in this and the next lesson, provide them each with a small copy of the names of each feature and an image next to it.

Extend the *Toolkit* Lesson

LANGUAGE PRACTICE
Writing and
Drawing Features

Students practice writing and drawing labels, captions, and other features. Students use images from a magazine, an online source, or their own illustrations. They label or write captions for their illustration, or write and draw different features, placing these on a class poster.

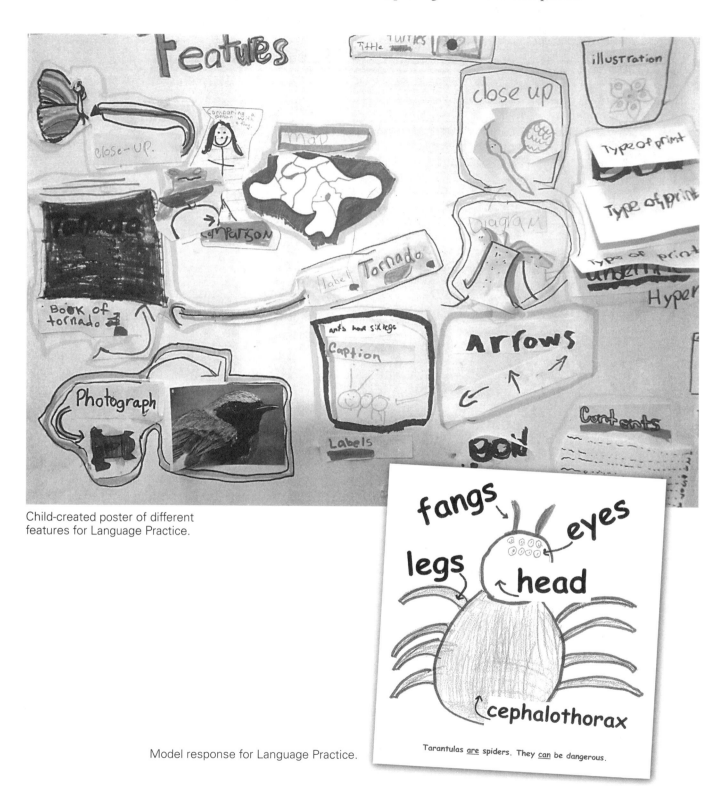

Child-created poster of different features for Language Practice.

Model response for Language Practice.

CONTENT AND COMPREHENSION EXTENSION

Kids create posters about a topic they know about. Support them to find information and decide which features they will use to share it. Using features in their own writing and drawing solidifies children's understanding of the ways in which features convey accurate information.

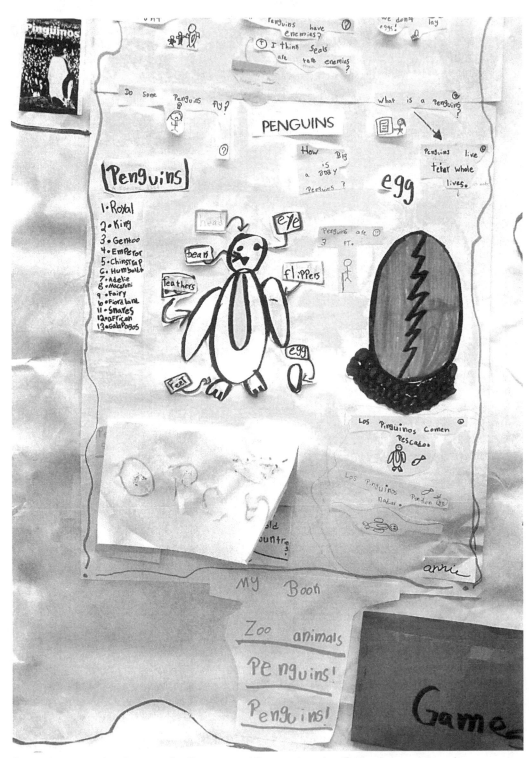

Poster incorporating features for Content and Comprehension Extension.

Creating posters with text features.

EXPLORE Nonfiction Features

Create *Nonfiction Feature* books

PREVIEW GOALS

We want students to

CONTENT	write and draw about their own topics or real-life experiences.
COMPREHENSION	understand how to use nonfiction features in writing and drawing.
LANGUAGE	practice writing and reading simple sentences.

KEY VOCABULARY

COMPREHENSION WORDS
all nonfiction feature vocabulary (*photographs, captions, labels,* etc.)

CONTENT WORDS
words related to the children's own topics

LANGUAGE STRUCTURES

Simple descriptive sentences facilitate discussion of text features.

This is a picture of _____. It is _____.

This is _____. It is _____ and _____.

This is a _____. It shows _____.

Preview the *Toolkit* Lesson

Continuing work with visual and text features, the Preview gives kids a head start on the *Toolkit* lesson.

Used with permission from *TIME For Kids*. From *National Geographic Young Explorer*. Reprinted by permission.

- Review the nonfiction features from the anchor chart created in *Toolkit* Lesson 2. Support kids by having examples of each of the features on display or easily referenced. Looking at the *TIME for Kids* poster "Taking a Trip" or the National Geographic *Fly with a Butterfly* magazine, have kids identify the features.

- Ask children to choose a visual feature to talk about. Start with a basic frame, and guide students to add to it. *This is a picture (illustration, map) of _____. It is _____.*

- One option is for children to write and draw about themselves, their families, their favorite foods, or their favorite activities. They write labels and captions to explain their illustrations.

Child's response from Preview.

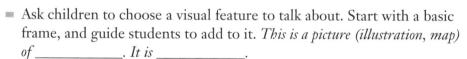

Writing Captions

This is a picture of _____. It is _____.

This is _____. It is _____ and _____.

This is a _____. It shows _____.

- As an additional support, provide students with a page of nonfiction features represented with images. (See the sample chart on page 26 of Lesson 3 in the *Toolkit* Monitoring Comprehension book.)

Teach the *Toolkit* Lesson

Make sure the sentence frames for describing pictures (the Writing Captions chart) and the nonfiction features anchor chart from *Toolkit Lesson 2* are easily visible during this lesson.

If students have begun work on their book about themselves during the Preview, encourage them to continue this during the Guide portion of the lesson. Remind them to look at the anchor chart for ideas for features to include.

Extend the *Toolkit* Lesson

LANGUAGE PRACTICE
Prepositions

Language practice with prepositions is fun, especially when kids can act them out. In this lesson, children view images of butterflies to help them talk about and then write descriptive sentences with prepositions.

Create an anchor chart with pictures of the butterflies illustrating prepositional captions, (for example, *on a twig, under a leaf, above a flower*). Leave the actual preposition as a blank space to be filled in later by the students.

Student work for Language Practice.

Write prepositions on cards or Post-its: *above, across, around, down, from, in, inside, off, on, out, outside, through, to, under, up.* Then act out and demonstrate them. For example, act out what a butterfly does: *Glide <u>around</u> the room. Flutter <u>up</u> and <u>down</u>. Land <u>on</u> the floor or <u>under</u> a desk. Fly <u>across</u> the room to sit <u>on</u> a "flower."*

Butterflies fly __in__ the forest.
Butterflies fly __above__ plants.
Butterflies flutter __through__ meadows.
Butterflies drink nectar __from__ the flowers.
Butterflies lay eggs __on__ leaves.
Chrysalis hang __from__ branches.
Caterpillars crawl __up__ trees.
Butterflies have antenna __on top of__ their heads.

forest
meadow ↓
leaf ↑
butterfly ↑
antenna ↓
caterpillar ↑
branch
chrysalis
nectar (juice from flower)

Anchor chart for Language Practice.

Pass out the preposition Post-its to students. Read the prepositional phrases on the chart, prompting the student who has the correct preposition on his or her Post-it to stick it into the blank space on the anchor chart.

Practice pronouncing, reading, and acting out each preposition as the students place them on the chart.

Release the children to draw and then write prepositional phrases.

The butterfly sits _____ the leaf.
The butterfly drinks nectar _____ a flower.
The butterfly flies _____ the forest.
The butterfly flutters _____ the wildflowers.
The butterfly lands _____ the garden.

CONTENT AND COMPREHENSION EXTENSION

To create a short PowerPoint presentation, kids work with a partner and choose a topic. They create a few blank slides and add photographs or other images to these. They can add labels, captions, and other features. Experimenting with colored fonts or even animations keeps kids interested and engaged in thinking about how they will use text and visual features to communicate information.

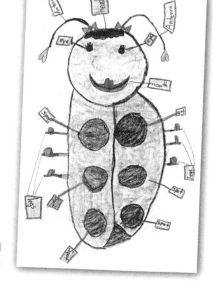

Child's work for Content and Comprehension Extension.

DISCOVER YOUR Passion

Become a specialist

PREVIEW GOALS

We want students to

CONTENT
- talk about and make a list of topics they know and care about.

COMPREHENSION
- understand what it means to know about a topic, care about it, and teach others about it.

LANGUAGE
- develop a repertoire of ways to express what they know about and care about.

KEY VOCABULARY

COMPREHENSION WORDS
specialist
topic
teach
passion
passionate
nonfiction feature
  vocabulary (*illustrations,*
  table of contents, etc.)
photo
label
glossary
index

CONTENT WORDS
words related to the
  children's own topics

LANGUAGE STRUCTURES

In preparation for students creating a list of topics that interest them during the *Toolkit* lesson, the Preview teaches language structures that signal what kids know a lot about and care about.

I know _____.

I learned that _____.

I know a lot about _____.

I like _____.

I love _____.

Preview the *Toolkit* Lesson

The Preview provides students with opportunities to talk in a small group about what they know and are passionate about in order to begin their own list of these topics.

- Everyone is a specialist—children know and care about many things.

- Refer back to Tommy in *The Art Lesson* (*Toolkit* Lesson 1), and point out that he is a specialist in art and that he is also passionate about it. Explain that being *passionate* means you like something a lot and care about it.

- Ask children to turn and talk about what they know and care about, what they are passionate about. It may be a certain pet, a special family member, or a favorite grandparent. Chart the language frames for the children to practice with on a What I Know and Like chart.

From *National Geographic Young Explorer.* Reprinted by permission.

What I Know and Like

I know _____.

I learned that _____.

I know a lot about _____.

I like _____.

I love _____.

- Explain to kids that they will teach others about what they know and care about, just as other authors do, and that they will be writing books that teach. Tell them that the first step is to think carefully about what they most want to write about.

- As students brainstorm what they know a lot about and care a lot about, chart these ideas and support kids to begin a list of topics to give them a head start on their books and the *Toolkit* lesson.

- Finish by having kids share out, providing model conversational moves for getting a dialogue going about their interests and passions: "I know a lot about _____. I know _____. What do you know a lot about?"

Teach the *Toolkit* Lesson

Post the language frames chart from the Preview and the features charts from Lessons 2 and 3 so that students can use these while talking and writing. Remind students who participated in the Preview to bring the lists of topics they created to the lesson. Children who have already put some thought into their topics could share these with the whole class.

During the Guide portion of the lesson, confer with students to identify one specialist topic they would like to write about.

Extend the *Toolkit* Lesson

LANGUAGE PRACTICE
Descriptive Language, the Conjunction *and*

Practicing descriptive language encourages kids to add more elaborate vocabulary and ideas to their teaching books. Kids often know a lot about sports and activities such as dancing, so we orally discuss verbs that describe different activities and add these to an anchor chart.

Anchor chart of descriptive language for Language Practice.

Create a four-column anchor chart with pictures of different activities and sports in the first column; then make three columns that follow a verb-and-verb pattern. Using sports-related verbs (for example, *twirl, leap, turn; jump, dribble, run; race, turn, stop*) written on Post-its as examples, ask children to look at each picture of an activity or sport and orally brainstorm additional verbs, or action words, that describe each activity or sport. Write these on Post-its, too. Work with the group to read each one and then compose a descriptive sentence following the pattern. For example, verbs that describe the ballet dancer might be: *Ballet dancers twirl and leap*. Kids can then place the appropriate verbs next to a particular activity or sport using the sentence frame. They can then reread the sentences and discuss action words that they come up with to broaden their vocabulary knowledge.

Soccer players ___run___ and ___kick balls___.

Ballet dancers ___twirl___ and ___Jump___.

Children's thinksheet for Language Practice.

To review, prepare language thinksheets with the language frame from the chart (have several copies of each activity or sport handy). Ask the children to write the words independently and illustrate the sentences, using the anchor chart as a reference.

CONTENT AND COMPREHENSION EXTENSION

Encourage children to explore books, magazines, and websites to investigate how other authors create interesting writing that teaches us information. Following are three author-based websites:

http://www.stevejenkinsbooks.com/

http://www.eric-carle.com/home.html

http://www.gailgibbons.com/

Look at interactive websites to notice what gets kids interested in a topic— and what authors do to make their topic engaging to the reader. Talk about what makes for interesting articles (lots of pictures, diagrams, labels, captions). Suggest that students check out these science-based websites:

http://www.nationalgeographic.com/ngyoungexplorer/

http://www.extremescience.com/zoom/index.php/animal-kingdom

http://kids.earth.nasa.gov/

http://solarsystem.nasa.gov/kids/index.cfm

THINK ABOUT What You Know

Write teaching books

PREVIEW GOALS

We want students to

CONTENT ■ write as specialists about themselves or a topic that they choose.

COMPREHENSION ■ apply knowledge of nonfiction features in their own texts.

LANGUAGE ■ use descriptive language to elaborate on and teach about topics.

KEY VOCABULARY

COMPREHENSION WORDS
accuracy
specialist
topic
all nonfiction feature
  vocabulary

CONTENT WORDS
words related to the
  children's own topics

LANGUAGE STRUCTURES

These language frames allow students to show what they know or are learning. During the *Toolkit* lesson, they take these language frames into writing.

I know _____.

I learned that _____.

I know a lot about _____.

I like _____ because _____.

I like _____ and _____.

I love _____.

Preview the *Toolkit* Lesson

From *National Geographic Young Explorer*. Reprinted by permission.

Toolkit Lesson 5 asks students to use one of the specialist topics from the lists they generated in Lesson 4 to create teaching books. In the Preview, help kids elaborate on their topics, deciding what they want to write and rehearsing orally before they try to get it down in writing and illustrate it during the *Toolkit* lesson.

- Guide kids to talk about three or four things they want to teach others about their topic. Review the concept of information and the idea that when we read nonfiction, we learn information. Help them write these thoughts on Post-its or sketch illustrations that teach the information.

- Build on the language structures introduced in Lesson 4, adding examples of conjunctions, such as *and* or *because*. Briefly model an example of how to draw and write a page about a topic.

What I Know and Like

I know _____.

I learned that _____.

I know a lot about _____.

I like _____ because _____.

I like _____ and _____.

I love _____.

- Support students who are ready to express their ideas in a slightly more complex form. They can still use the simple sentence structures, but challenge them to extend those by using the conjunctions *and* or *because*. For example:

> I like soccer because it is fun to be outside and play with my friends.
> I have soccer shoes and a soccer ball.
> I like to run fast and score a goal!
>
> I know a lot about rattlesnakes.
> Rattlesnakes are reptiles.
> Rattlesnakes slither and rattle.
> Rattlesnakes are poisonous and dangerous.

- Confer with individual students to elaborate on their ideas—scribing their ideas on Post-its if it's helpful to capture the children's voices. The Post-its serve as a rehearsal, a way for kids to get their thinking down, and will guide their writing. They serve as a plan that will support kids to write and draw during the independent part of the whole-group lesson.

Teach the *Toolkit* Lesson

Make sure the What I Know and Like language frames from the Preview for Lesson 4 and 5 are posted so that students can use these in their writing.

During independent practice, encourage students to take each Post-it they created during the Preview and write about it on one page. Confer with them as they write so they are clear about how to go from recording their thinking on Post-its to writing their thoughts in complete sentences.

Give the students who are writing in a new language ample time to add their illustrations before asking them to share out during Share the Learning.

TOOLKIT GOALS

We want students to

- understand the term *accuracy* and apply it to their teaching book.
- write teaching books on topics that they know and care a lot about.
- include nonfiction visual and text features as well as written text in their teaching books.

What Do Penguins Eat?

Penguins eat fish. I wonder what else they eat?

Child's page from a teaching book.

Extend the *Toolkit* Lesson

LANGUAGE PRACTICE
Elaboration

For additional writing and drawing practice, show kids ways to make their writing more interesting and informative. Make a two-column chart with the headings "Simple Sentences" on one side and "More Elaborate Sentences" on the other. Any topic is fine. Here we used cheetahs as the example. Write the simple sentence first, and then brainstorm with the kids about ways to make the sentence more interesting and exciting. As you write the sentences, draw pictures to go along with them to provide visual cues.

Simple Sentences	More Elaborate Sentences
Cheetahs run fast.	Cheetahs are some of fastest cats on Earth!
Cheetahs have black spots.	Cheetahs have black spots that help camouflage them in the grass.
Cheetahs hunt.	Cheetahs are patient hunters—they wait to pounce on their prey.

Once the whole group has practiced, give the kids time to write two of their own sentences—one a simple sentence, the second a more elaborate version of the same—and illustrate them.

CONTENT AND COMPREHENSION EXTENSION

To create a home-school connection, send a letter home in students' home language(s) explaining that the project will teach kids to use nonfiction features such as drawing, labeling, and writing captions to write about themselves and their lives—what they are experts in (for example, cooking), what their home countries or languages are like, or what games they like to play. Ask family members to discuss aspects of the students' lives in their home languages and communities that they can then use to write their books at school.

Children write about their lives and interests.

Curry is made from coconut milk and is spicy and hot. You take roti and dip and scoop it into the curry. It is so good!

Are you hungry for Indian food now? I am!

Lunch In India

Written and Illustrated by Subhangi

This book is for my family.

Lunch and Eating

Did you know that Indian food is really good? It is!

Do you like to eat lunch? So do people in India?

Roti is bread that is really good. You use roti to scoop up food and eat it! It's delicious!

In India banana leaves are used for plates. That's cool!

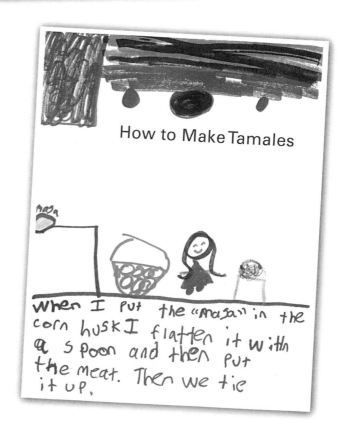

How to Make Tamales

masa

When I put the "masa" in the corn husk I flatten it with a spoon and then put the meat. Then we tie it up.

MAKE Connections

Use personal experience to construct meaning

PREVIEW GOALS

We want students to

CONTENT ▪ understand the concepts in the story in order to make connections with the text, especially solving a problem.

COMPREHENSION ▪ establish an understanding of the text by connecting to and empathizing with the character's predicament.

LANGUAGE ▪ be able to transfer the information from their inner voice in their native language to English in order to communicate their thinking.

KEY VOCABULARY

COMPREHENSION WORDS
connection
inner voice
reminds me of

CONTENT WORDS
lost
found
sad
worried

LANGUAGE STRUCTURES

The Preview gives students ways to talk and write about their connections. The language frame *This helps me understand because _____.* supports kids to explain and elaborate on their connections.

When I _____, I felt _____.
When I lost my cat, I felt sad.

This reminds me of _____.
This reminds me of when I lost my cat.

I have a connection because _____.
I have a connection because I once lost my cat.

This helps me understand because _____.
This helps me understand because I once lost my cat and we made posters to look for it.

Preview the *Toolkit* Lesson

The Preview makes sure children understand a key idea in the story for the *Toolkit* lesson (the concept of having lost something) and introduces them to the language of making connections.

- Hold up the cover of *Patches Lost and Found*, and read the title aloud. Ask children, *What do you see? What do you think the book will be about?* Discuss the idea of losing something, and talk about how the girl probably feels, probably sad or worried.

- Encourage kids to talk about something they have lost. Introduce the concept of the inner voice. Explain that this is the voice in their heads, what they are thinking about. Remember that some children may be listening to an inner voice that is in their heritage language and that they will be transferring this talk from one language to another when they speak and write.

- Post the language frame *When I lost _____, I felt _____.* and provide several oral models (for example, "When I lost my backpack, I felt upset"). Then give students time to work on drawing an image of when they lost something and write what that was. Post the words and images on the chart.

- Use the language structures chart to review and expand on the language of making connections. Tell the students that when they hear themselves say, *This reminds me of _____*, they are making a connection! That's what they will be doing in the whole-group *Toolkit* lesson.

Anchor chart for feelings.

Making Connections

When I _____, I felt _____.

This reminds me of _____.

I have a connection because _____.

This helps me understand because _____.

- To teach students to explain how their connection helped them understand the text, introduce and work with the frame *This helps me understand because _____.*

Teach the *Toolkit* Lesson

Post the language structures charts from the Preview for students to use as a reference during the *Toolkit* lesson. A thinksheet containing the language frames provides support for their writing.

To support new learners of English during the Guide portion of the lesson, check in with them briefly to help them verbalize their thinking before writing it down. During the Practice Independently section, confer with students to prompt oral answers before asking them to write or draw a connection: "How are you like Jenny?" "How is someone you know like Mr. Griswold? Like Jenny's mom? Like Mr. Scooter?"

Extend the *Toolkit* Lesson

LANGUAGE PRACTICE
Singular and Plural Nouns

The idea of countable nouns in English is different from other language systems. It is important to explicitly practice singular and plural forms of nouns so students begin to distinguish their pronunciations and spellings.

Regular countable nouns are changed by adding *-s* or *-es* to the singular form.

table	tables
pencil	pencils
chair	chairs
door	doors
box	boxes

If the word ends in a consonant plus *-y*, *y* is dropped and the ending is changed to *-ies*.

puppy	puppies
kitty	kitties
bully	bullies
story	stories

Irregular countable nouns become plurals by changing the letters. Following are some examples.

mouse	mice
foot	feet
child	children

Divide chart paper into two sections: a top section for nouns with regular plurals, a bottom section for nouns with irregular plurals. At the top, write a column of singular nouns and a second column with their matching regular plural nouns. Do the same for nouns with irregular plurals. When you are writing plurals, make it clear how the root noun changes so that the spelling is visible to the students.

Explain that a noun is a person, place, or thing. Give real examples, and use either pictures or real objects to demonstrate the meaning of all the nouns and their plurals. (Using pets to start with helps connect the lesson to *Patches*.)

Make noun cards in both singular and plural forms. Mix the cards up, and pass them out to the students. Guide the students to go up to the chart and match the cards to the nouns on the chart. Then ask children to work independently to illustrate and write sample nouns, talking about their words with a partner. For example, have them draw images of one puppy with a space below to write the word *puppy* and then another image with multiple puppies for them to label *puppies*.

Singular Nouns/Plural Nouns anchor chart.

CONTENT AND COMPREHENSION EXTENSION

Encourage students to write stories—first drawing pictures and then writing—just as Jenny in the story *Patches* did. Reread the story and use Jenny as the teaching model for narrating a story in art and then in words. Next, have children decide on a story they want to tell, and help them plan the events they want to draw. This is an excellent writing strategy for children learning English as they can organize their thinking through the pictures and then put the story into their new language.

MERGE THINKING with New Learning

Stop, think, and react to information

PREVIEW GOALS

We want students to

CONTENT
- activate and develop background knowledge and vocabulary about insects.

COMPREHENSION
- use background knowledge to build from known facts and gain new knowledge.

LANGUAGE
- learn and use language for reacting and responding to new information. ("Wow!" "Amazing!" "I never knew that!")
- talk about both background knowledge and new information.

KEY VOCABULARY

COMPREHENSION WORDS
new learning
merge
respond
react
background knowledge

CONTENT WORDS
grasshopper
praying mantis
fly
katydid
bee
wing
leg
body
head
mouth

LANGUAGE STRUCTURES

To prepare for the *Toolkit* lesson's work with background knowledge and new learning, the Preview provides language for expressing both and reviews some language for making connections.

I know _____.
I know insects have six legs.

I learned that _____.
I learned that some insects have wings.

Wow! _____.
It's amazing that _____!
This reminds me of _____.
I didn't know _____!
I never knew that _____!

Preview the *Toolkit* Lesson

To rehearse for the *Toolkit* lesson, children learn new information about insects and merge their new learning with what they already know.

■ Hold up the cover of the book *Insects*, and explain that the photograph shows a grasshopper, one kind of insect or bug. Ask kids to turn and talk about what they already know about insects. Explain that what they already know is their background knowledge, or BK.

■ Ask the students to turn and talk about what they learned about insects or about a connection they have to the world of insects. Model an example and ask them to write or draw their thinking on a Post-it using the appropriate language frame.

From *Insects* by Robin Bernard. Copyright © 1999. Reprinted by permission of National Geographic Society.

New Learning

I know _____.

I learned that _____.

Wow! _____.

It's amazing that _____!

This reminds me of _____.

I didn't know _____!

I never knew that _____!

■ Return to the *Insects* cover, and have kids help you label the parts of the grasshopper: head, body, feelers, legs, wings.

■ Choose a page to read aloud and ask students to respond to the photographs and text using the language structures (*I know, I learned*). Model how to merge what you already know with new information.

Labels of the parts of the grasshopper for Preview.

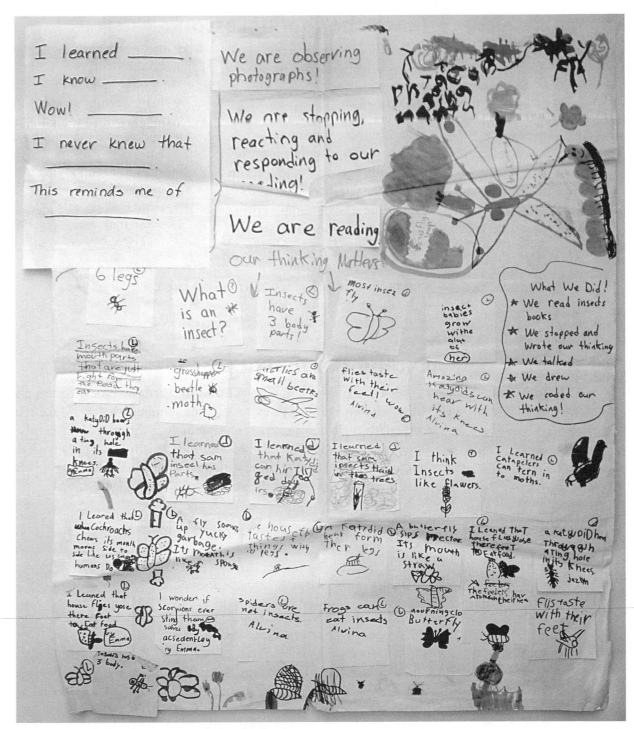

Anchor chart of student responses during the Preview.

- Model a reaction, such as "Wow! Katydids have their 'ears' in their knees! I never knew that!" Ask kids to draw and write their own learning or reactions on a Post-it.

- Collect student responses and Post-its on an anchor chart.

Teach the *Toolkit* Lesson

Post the language structures chart for students to use during the lesson when kids are responding to the pictures and text.

As children are practicing independently, you may want to direct kids back to the lesson text or another familiar book on the same topic so they can practice writing information with which they are already comfortable. Consider writing the sentence frames from the Preview language structures chart on sentence strips that kids can pull off the chart or board to use for writing.

Extend the *Toolkit* Lesson

LANGUAGE PRACTICE
Comparing and Contrasting

Practice the language used to contrast different insects. Create a chart with the language structures and sample sentences below. Make sentence strips with the language structures (sentences with the blanks) only. Write additional contrasting sentences with the students, and then have them practice reading the sentences with a partner. Finally, have them choose a sentence and draw what the sentence is describing.

_____ is _____, but _____ is not.
An ant is an insect, but a spider is not.

_____ has _____, but _____ does not.
A butterfly has wings, but a spider does not.

_____ can _____. However, _____ cannot.
Flies can fly. However, cockroaches cannot.

The words in these frames that signal differences are *but* and *however* as well as the contrasting verbs *is/is not*, *has/does not*, and *can/cannot*.

Use two simple sentences to compare and contrast insects:

Butterflies can fly. Ants cannot fly.

Bees are insects. Spiders are not insects.

bee hive

mosquito

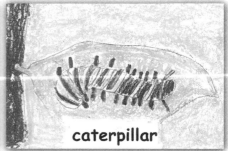
caterpillar

Images students created to compare and contrast insects during Language Practice.

Name: _____

Wasps can Fly
caterpillar cannot.

Fireflies have a light
Bees do not have one

Mosquitoes are strong
Butterflies are not.

A praying mantis is big
A ladybug is not big

Name: _____

Butterfly can fly
caterpillar cannot.

Butterflies have wings
Caterpillars do not have wings

Butterflies are insects
Caterpillars are not.

A Butterfly is big
A Caterpillar is not big

Student responses from Language Practice session.

CONTENT AND COMPREHENSION EXTENSION

Co-construct a chart of the parts and behaviors of different insects in order to build children's knowledge about the ways in which insects are adapted to their environments. Children can use the books and articles collected for the *Toolkit* lesson as well as the resources in *The Primary Comprehension Toolkit*: the *TIME for Kids* ladybug poster, the *Insects* trade book, and the National Geographic *Young Explorer* magazine on butterflies. Or look online for photos and information appropriate for young learners.

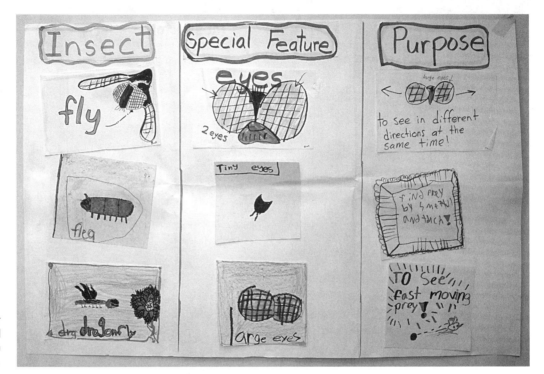

Anchor chart for the Content and Comprehension Extension.

Identify two or three insects to research, and help kids research and decide which facts to record on the chart. Demonstrate how to draw images for each section of the chart so that kids can communicate the information they are using visually as well as in writing.

Insect	Part	Action	Image
praying mantis	legs, strong jaw	It eats a grasshopper. Chameleons eat them! jumps fast to catch its prey	
grasshopper	legs mouth	jump to move chirps to communicate chews food	
butterfly	mouth long tongue like a circle wings	sips nectar acts like a straw can fly	

VIEW and READ to Learn and Wonder

Use images
and words
to gain
understanding

PREVIEW GOALS

We want students to

CONTENT
- use text and images to build content knowledge around a topic.

COMPREHENSION
- distinguish between learning new information and asking questions.
- understand how to organize their thinking in a two-column format.

LANGUAGE
- answer questions using their own background knowledge or new learning.

KEY VOCABULARY

COMPREHENSION WORDS
I know
I learned
I wonder
I think

CONTENT WORDS
spiders
legs
head
body
trap door spider
water spider
jumping spider

LANGUAGE STRUCTURES

These language frames expand ways for students to express background
knowledge and new learning as well as to ask questions.

I know _____.
I think _____.
I think I know _____.

I learned _____.
I wonder _____.
I used to think _____, but now I know _____.
I never knew _____.

Preview the *Toolkit* Lesson

Continuing with the bugs theme, the Preview—like the *Toolkit* lesson—focuses on spiders but doesn't give away the real surprise: Spiders are not insects!

■ Show children the *TIME for Kids* "Spiders!" poster, and ask them to think about what they already know, or think they know, about spiders. Then have them turn and talk about their knowledge using the first three language frames on the Knowing and Learning chart.

Used with permission from *TIME for Kids*.

Knowing and Learning

I know _____.

I think _____.

I think I know _____.

I learned _____.

I wonder _____.

I used to think _____, but now I know _____.

I never knew _____.

■ Ask students to draw and write what they know or think they know on Post-its and then share out, using the language frames.

■ Display page 4 of the *TIME for Kids* poster "Spiders!" Talk about the body parts of the spider. Together, look at the illustration.

■ Ask kids if they learned anything new about spiders. Reinforce the language that describes new learning: *I learned that _____. I never knew _____.*

■ Explain that when we learn new information, we often have a question about it. We say, "I wonder _____." Using the photograph, model several "I wonder" statements about spiders. Emphasize the difference between information learned and information questioned. Then ask kids to turn and talk about something they learned or something they wonder about spiders.

■ To wrap up, have students act out the ways they think spiders move: jump, hop, crawl, and sneak.

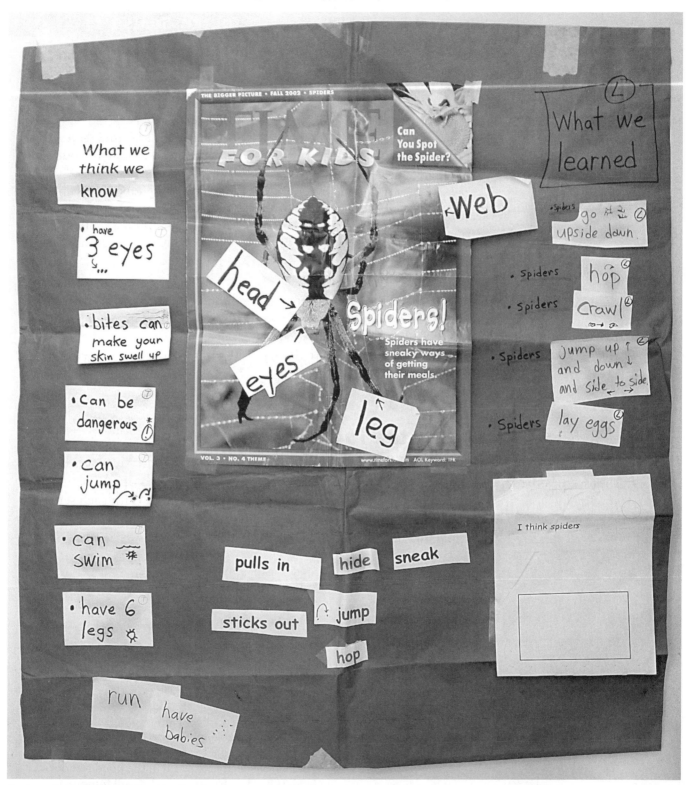

Anchor chart created during the Preview.

Teach the *Toolkit* Lesson

Post the language structures chart from the Preview, and prompt students to use it when sharing their knowledge of spiders in Connect and Engage.

As kids practice viewing and reading information during Guide and Collaborate, make sure they are distinguishing between what they are learning and what they are wondering.

To check for understanding as you confer, ask, "What have you learned today?" Also articulate what you notice the students are doing by saying things like "I saw you writing your thinking about spiders," "I saw you talking with each other about what you learned," and "I saw you draw your spider thinking." Comments like these support students to articulate their learning process.

> **TOOLKIT GOALS**
>
> **We want students to**
> - use text and images to understand.
> - think and wonder about new learning.
> - jot down new learning and questions on Post-its, and then sort them in two columns: *I Learned* and *I Wonder*.
> - understand that misconceptions are normal and that learners revise their thinking after reading and listening to additional information.

Extend the *Toolkit* Lesson

LANGUAGE PRACTICE
The Modal Verb *can*

The modal auxiliary *can* is helpful for children to practice since it is both useful and irregular. The present, past, and future tenses of *can* change unpredictably. Present the examples in the chart below. With each sentence, sketch or have the kids sketch the spider's action. For example, draw a spider jumping for the sentence *Spiders can jump.*

present	can	Spiders <u>can</u> jump. Spiders <u>can</u> crawl. Spiders <u>can</u> swim. Spiders <u>can</u> climb.	
past	could	I saw a spider that <u>could</u> jump. I saw a spider that <u>could</u> crawl. I saw a spider that <u>could</u> swim. I saw a spider that <u>could</u> climb.	
future	will be able to	Spiders <u>will be able to</u> jump in the garden tomorrow. Spiders <u>will be able to</u> crawl on the plant tomorrow. Spiders <u>will be able to</u> swim in the pond tomorrow. Spiders <u>will be able to</u> climb the wall tomorrow.	

Read the present tense sentences. Pose and post the question, "What can spiders do?" Pair up the kids, and have one student ask the other to answer the question using the chart or making up his or her own answers using the modal verb *can*.

Read the past tense sentences, and pose and post the question, "What did you see?" Again, have students ask and answer each other.

Follow the same procedure with the future tense examples.

CONTENT AND COMPREHENSION EXTENSION

Encourage children to create self-published books or informational poems about a topic they are learning about. Give them a simple set of directions, illustrated to make the steps clear.

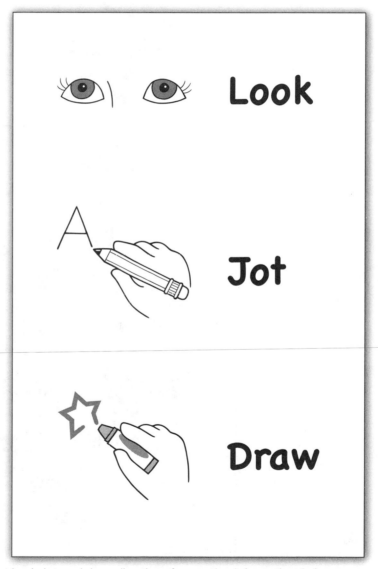

Look, jot, and draw directions for creating informational pieces.

When they are ready to write, help them illustrate and translate their information to the book pages using the language structures and thinking strategies in this lesson. Or kids can write their information as lines in a free verse poem and illustrate. Provide an opportunity for kids to read their books or poems to each other and to write and draw comments about each other's work.

Poem capturing insect information for the Content and Comprehension Extension.

WONDER ABOUT New Information

Ask questions when you read, listen, and view

PREVIEW GOALS

We want students to

CONTENT
- build background knowledge and vocabulary around a topic.

COMPREHENSION
- practice asking a question using an open-ended format.
- understand vocabulary words: *curious, wonder, lingering question*.

LANGUAGE
- review and practice how to phrase a question.
- use words that signal questions: *how, what*.

KEY VOCABULARY

COMPREHENSION WORDS
wonder
curious
lingering question

CONTENT WORDS
snow
cold
thermometer
Arctic Circle
Alaska
recess
winter clothing (parka,
  snow pants, hat, mittens,
  gloves, scarf)

LANGUAGE STRUCTURES

The following language frames for questioning are the foundation for all the Ask Questions lessons.

I wonder _____ .
How _____ ?
What _____ ?
Why _____ ?
Where _____ ?
Who _____ ?
When _____ ?

Preview the *Toolkit* Lesson

The Preview develops background knowledge of the Arctic so that kids will better understand the *Toolkit* lesson text.

- Use a globe to enhance understanding of where *Recess at 20 Below* takes place, especially the location of Alaska in the far north and the location of the Arctic Circle. (Another option is to go to http://earth.google.com/ for locating and learning about Alaska.)

- Ask kids to turn and talk about their background knowledge about cold places. Discuss related concepts and vocabulary: *snow, cold, thermometer, Arctic Circle, Alaska,* and *winter clothing* to introduce vocabulary. Kids try on and talk about winter clothing.

From *Recess at 20 Below* by Cindy Lou Aillaud, © 2005, used with permission from Alaska Northwest Books ®, an imprint of Graphic Arts Center Publishing Company.

← hat

scarf →

parka →

snow pants →

Our <u>background knowledge</u> (BK) about Alaska and what it is like to live in a very cold place!

Animals, like moose, live in Alaska!

We know kids wear a <u>lot</u> of clothes to play outside in Alaska

We <u>think</u> some people live in the Arctic, where it is very cold.

Anchor charts for Preview.

← mittens

- Introduce the language stems for asking a question using the Asking Questions language structures chart.

Asking Questions

I wonder _____.

How _____?

What _____?

Why _____?

Where _____?

Who _____?

When _____?

- Remind students that they already know *I wonder* _____ signals a question. Model questions about life in Alaska using the question words. Share the language of being curious—explain to kids that when we want to find things out, we are curious and we ask a lot of questions.

- Guide students to think about any questions they have about Alaska, and post these on an anchor chart. Emphasize how curious they are, referring to the many questions they have already begun to ask.

- Give children an opportunity to page through the first few pages of the book, asking questions about anything they are curious about. As children ask questions about the photographs they see, have them turn and talk and share out their questions.

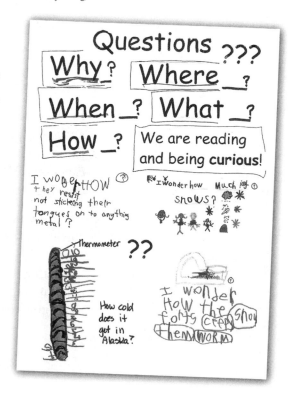

- Ask kids to write or draw their questions on Post-its and stick these on the anchor chart. Suggest that kids may be able to answer some of their questions when they read the book during the *Toolkit* lesson.

Anchor chart for Preview.

Teach the *Toolkit* Lesson

Post the language structures chart and the anchor chart of kids' questions about Alaska and the Arctic so kids can refer to them during the lesson. During the Practice Independently section, circle back around to the Preview students to see if any of their questions were answered and identify those that were not (that is, the lingering questions).

Children can use the question Post-its on their anchor chart to participate in Share the Learning, explaining what they are still curious about.

Extend the *Toolkit* Lesson

LANGUAGE PRACTICE
Opposites

Antonym practice helps build vocabulary and allows students to verbalize their thinking when comparing and contrasting information.

Create pairs of word cards with an image for each antonym, or opposite. The following list contains words with antonyms from *Recess at 20 Below*.

cold–hot	long–short	first–last	throw–catch
cool–warm	out–in	outside–inside	hard–soft
pull–push	a lot–a little	high–low	thick–thin
on–off	thick–thin	top–bottom	heavy–light
up–down	winter–summer	soft–hard	light–dark
in–out	put on–take off	easy–hard	cloudy–sunny

In class, begin with a two-column chart titled "Antonyms." Define the word *antonyms* (opposites) at the top of the chart, and discuss what an antonym is. Bring students up to model several pairs—perhaps *tall–short*, *run–walk*, or *happy–sad*. Write these antonyms as examples on the chart, and include quick drawings to show the contrasts.

Then divide students into two groups, giving one word in each antonym pair to children in one group and the other word in the pair to the other group. Have everyone look for her or his antonym pair in the other group. Once they've found each other, have them sit down. As a group, add the pairs of antonyms to the chart, act out each antonym, and verbally rehearse its pronunciation.

As an extension, the students can make antonym books—an opportunity for differentiation. Emergent learners may simply write the antonym and draw a representative image. More advanced learners can be challenged to create sentences about *Recess at 20 Below* to practice the antonyms in context. For example: *Recess in Alaska can be <u>cold</u>, but in Colorado it is sometimes <u>hot</u>.*

Alaska is __Cold__ and Mexico is __hot__.

Student work for Language Practice.

CONTENT AND COMPREHENSION EXTENSION

Search for picture books and online resources about Alaska and the Arctic to extend kids' work on finding answers to lingering questions. Encourage children to explore these resources, and help them think about ways they might find the answers to their questions. Support kids to notice as their questions are answered by viewing photographs and reading on for more information. On their lingering questions anchor chart, they can post an answer near their question and link questions and answers with an arrow.

USE QUESTIONS as Tools for Learning

Understand why some questions are answered and some are not

PREVIEW GOALS

We want students to

CONTENT
- ask and answer questions about the content, using an image or text.

COMPREHENSION
- learn and understand that there are different ways to ask and answer questions—by viewing, reading, and talking.

LANGUAGE
- practice asking a question and answering it.
- practice using adjectives and their superlatives to describe animals.

KEY VOCABULARY

COMPREHENSION WORDS
ask
answer
view
read
talk

CONTENT WORDS
superlatives defined in
the context of the lesson
text (*biggest, smallest,
strongest*, etc.)

LANGUAGE STRUCTURES

The syntax, or word order, for asking questions can often be confusing for English language learners if the syntax of the children's home language differs from that of English. The Preview provides more practice with asking questions and adds the phrase *I learned* _____ for answering questions.

I wonder _____.
How _____?
What does/do _____?
Why _____?
Where _____?
Who _____?
When does/do _____?

I learned _____.

Preview the *Toolkit* Lesson

In this Preview, students practice asking and answering questions about animals in the book.

Excerpt from *Biggest, Strongest, Fastest* by Steve Jenkins. Copyright © 1995 by Steve Jenkins. Reprinted by permission of Houghton Mifflin Company. All rights reserved.

- Page through *Biggest, Strongest, Fastest* (also available in Spanish) to help children become familiar with the animals depicted. Ask kids to talk about what they think they know about some of the animals.

- Post a chart with the language frames for asking and answering questions, and remind children that they have asked questions before. Now we are going to search for and talk about the information that answers questions.

Asking and Answering Questions

I wonder _____.

How _____?

What does/do _____?

Why _____?

Where _____?

Who _____?

When does/do _____?

I learned _____.

- Return to *Biggest, Fastest, Strongest*, showing kids the pictures of animals and insects, and ask them which ones they wonder about. Have them turn and talk about something they wonder about the animals. Ask children to share out with the group.

- Write students' questions on Post-its or an anchor chart. Once they've finished questioning, work together to look for some answers, reading and looking at the pictures on the relevant pages. Explain that we view, read, and talk to answer our questions. Whether their questions are answered or not, at the end of each page, ask children, "What did you learn?" and have them answer using the *I learned* _____ language stem.

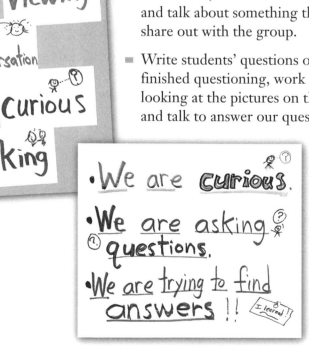

Anchor charts for Preview.

Teach the *Toolkit* Lesson

Post the Asking and Answering Questions language structures chart where children can refer to it during the lesson when kids are responding to and generating questions about the text. Adding sketched images to the questions and answers written on the two-column Questions/Answers chart in Lesson 10 will support children's comprehension during the lesson, as will using arrows to connect a question with an appropriate answer.

Extend the *Toolkit* Lesson

LANGUAGE PRACTICE
Comparative Adjectives

The book *Biggest, Strongest, Fastest* uses superlative forms of adjectives. Take this opportunity to work on the comparative forms of the same adjectives—*bigger, stronger, faster, smaller, slower, longer, taller, larger*—and reinforce the relationships introduced in the book. Make vocabulary word cards or Post-its containing each of these adjectives. Display images of the book animals on a chart or poster, and write a language frame with the comparative adjective missing underneath each one. For example, under the picture of the elephant, write:

Elephants are _____ than snails.

Pass out vocabulary word cards with the adjectives, and ask students who have the appropriate adjectives to place their cards in the blank. (*Elephants are bigger/taller/faster than snails.*) As a group, decide which word you want to complete the sentences. Finally, do a shared reading of each sentence.

We are using comparative adjectives!
Elephants are ___bigger___ than snails.
Giraffes are ___taller___ than people.
Cheetahs are ___faster___ than wild dogs.
Anacondas are ___longer___ than boas.
Blue whales are ___heavier___ than dolphins.
Hummingbirds are ___smaller___ than eagles.
Etruscan shrews are ___slower___ than lions.

Comparative adjectives include:
bigger   smaller   lighter
faster   heavier   longer
shorter   taller   slower

Anchor chart for Language Practice.

Student work for Language Practice.

Check out Steve Jenkins' book *Actual Size*, which illustrates the actual sizes of some amazing animals. After sharing this book, a fun, hands-on extension is to measure the heights and lengths of different animals. Starting with animals in the lesson text, such as the 25-foot-long anaconda, or the tiny Etruscan shrew, find the animal's length on a tape measure or yardstick and roll out masking tape on the floor to match the length or height of each animal. Add a label describing its size and unusual characteristics; include an illustration of the animal to bring this "actual size display" to life.

READ with a Question in Mind

Find answers to expand thinking

PREVIEW GOALS

We want students to

CONTENT
- learn information and answer questions using features such as photos, captions, and diagrams, in this case to expand understanding of extreme weather.

COMPREHENSION
- read with a question in mind.
- practice different ways to answer questions—through talking and discussion, activating background knowledge, and reading the text.

LANGUAGE
- use descriptive language to describe a topic (extreme weather).

KEY VOCABULARY

COMPREHENSION WORDS
question
read with a question
 in mind

CONTENT WORDS
tornado
funnel of wind
towering clouds
dust
debris
damage
storm clouds

LANGUAGE STRUCTURES

The Preview reviews the structure for asking questions from Lessons 9 and 10.

I wonder _____.
How _____?
What does/do _____?
Why _____?
Where _____?
Who _____?
When does/do _____?

I learned _____.

Preview the *Toolkit* Lesson

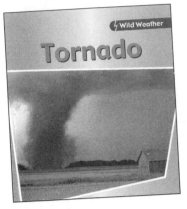

From *Tornado* by Catherine Chambers. Copyright © 2007. Reprinted by permission of Pearson Education.

- Show children the photographs of tornadoes on pages 4 and 5 and pages 12 and 13 of *Wild Weather: Tornado.* Ask kids to turn and talk about what they think they know about tornadoes and other severe weather events. (Alternatively, you can activate background knowledge by having kids look at photographs, videos, images, online sources, or video streaming to provide compelling visuals and information.)

- Co-construct an anchor chart with vocabulary and images about severe weather. Direct kids to write phrases and draw images for *storm clouds, towering clouds, spinning funnel, damage,* and so on. Act out the words *swirling, spinning,* and *windy* to convey the meaning of *tornado.* Bring in grass, sticks, and dirt to demonstrate the meaning of *debris.*

- Post children's words and images along with any other pictures and phrases you have gathered on the anchor chart. As an option for students who are ready to use the present progressive tense, practice describing the tornadoes using this tense.

- Post these present progressive frames:

    The tornado is _____. (spinning)

    The winds are _____. (blowing and shrieking)

- Review how to ask questions with the children, and use the same chart used in Lesson 9. Show them how to keep a question in mind as you read. Encourage children to ask questions about tornadoes that they think might be answered in the book and write them on a chart or board.

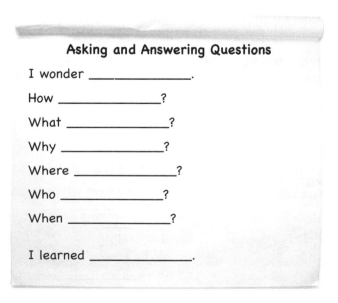

Anchor chart for Preview.

- Choose one of the questions children have asked, and briefly show how to find the answer to it using the photographs, text, and other features in *Wild Weather: Tornado*. Demonstrate how to write an answer if you can find one. If you do not find an answer, explain that our questions are not always answered. Kids will be asking and answering questions during the *Toolkit* lesson and need to know how to do both.

Teach the *Toolkit* Lesson

Post the language frames for asking and answering questions, the vocabulary anchor chart, and the chart of children's questions about tornadoes so kids can refer to them during the lesson.

While students are looking for answers, help kids out by restating questions to increase the likelihood that they will find an answer. This will help clarify the relationship between a reader's questions and information in the text as well as facilitate the research process.

Extend the *Toolkit* Lesson

LANGUAGE PRACTICE
The Verb *happen*

Wild Weather: Tornado poses a question using the word *happen*: *Where do tornadoes happen?* The use of *happen* to phrase questions can be confusing to speakers of other languages, so it is helpful to provide students with practice in the context of the lesson so that its significance is clear.

These are questions using the word "happen."	Write a response using the word "happen."	Do a drawing to show your thinking here.
Where do tornadoes happen?	Tornadoes happen in Tornado alley.	
How do they happen?	Tornadoes happen when cold and hot air crash together.	
Why do they happen?	Tornados happen because there is a big storm.	

New Words About Tornadoes:

		cold / Hot	
Tornado Alley	Funnel	Hot and Cold Air Merging	Lightning

Anchor chart for Language Practice.

Post the question *What is happening?* Begin by discussing what the word *happen* means (it means "occur" or even that "something is going on"). Display several images from *Wild Weather: Tornado*, and have children use the following frames to discuss extreme weather.

Where do _____ happen?   They happen in _____.

How do _____ happen?   They _____.

Why do _____ happen?   They happen because _____.

CONTENT AND COMPREHENSION EXTENSION

The vivid descriptive language that kids use to describe extreme weather is a natural for extending kids' learning and thinking into poetry. Using the vocabulary introduced in the Preview and expanded on in the lesson, kids can create their own extreme weather poems.

Child's tornado poem for Content and Comprehension Extension

Gather photographs and illustrations of extreme weather that prompt kids to use adjectives, verbs, and adverbs to describe what's going on: *spinning funnels*, *dark billowing clouds*, *lightning flashing across the sky*, *powerful screaming winds*. Encourage kids to use their senses—sight, sound, and movement—to create poems using descriptive language and to draw or sketch images representing their thinking.

To expand vocabulary on one weather topic (such as tornadoes), post a photograph and then write words that describe it. This supports children who are learning English to be more precise in their descriptions as well as building their vocabulary about the content.

Kids look at diagrams and illustrations to learn about a topic.

INFER Meaning

Merge background knowledge with clues from the text

PREVIEW GOALS

We want students to

CONTENT — learn that poetry can be abstract and requires inferring and interpretation.

COMPREHENSION — express their understanding of a poem through talking, writing, drawing, and dramatizing.

— understand that inferring takes different forms—visualizing and creating images, writing, and dramatizing.

LANGUAGE — use the language of inferring to talk, write, draw, and dramatize to make meaning with poetry.

KEY VOCABULARY

COMPREHENSION WORDS
infer
poems
poetry

CONTENT WORDS
words related to the
  poems to be read

LANGUAGE STRUCTURES

To begin the Infer and Visualize strategy, the Preview establishes two language frames for inferring:

I infer _____.

I think _____.

Preview the *Toolkit* Lesson

- To introduce the concept of inferring, have kids act out and infer emotions. Write emotion words (ranging from simple to more sophisticated words that describe emotions—for example, *mad, sad, happy, impatient, grumpy*) on slips of paper, or whisper the words to the actors. Have a child act out an emotion while his or her peers infer the emotion the child is portraying. Point out to the kids that they used a clue to figure out what the emotion was: the facial expression, the way someone acted, or the tone of voice.

- Discuss what the children just did—inferred, or figured out, what the person was feeling by looking and listening for clues. Write the stem *We inferred _____* on a chart, and expand it by describing what the students did: *We inferred that Ana was mad. We inferred that Anita was happy.* Draw a quick sketch to reinforce the meaning of the word or emotion, and ask kids to illustrate one of the emotions to demonstrate its meaning.

- To extend the meaning of *infer* in the text, read aloud and talk about the poem "Butterfly" on page 48 of the *Keep Reading!* source book. Read the poem two lines at a time, asking kids to infer what is going on. Prompt them with questions like these: "Why is the butterfly looking for a spot?" "What clues helped you figure that out?" Have them use the language frames to begin their response: *I infer that she's looking for a place to lay her eggs. I think that because then she lays her eggs under a leaf.*

Inferring

I infer _____.

I think _____.

Teach the *Toolkit* Lesson

Post the language frames for inferring for kids to use throughout the lesson.

Refer to the poem "Things" on the chart paper so that when you are doing the echo read, you can point to the words that the children are to repeat.

TOOLKIT GOALS

We want students to

- understand what it means to infer.
- infer the meaning of poems by merging their background knowledge with clues from the text.
- grow to cherish the sound of words and the rhythm of language.

Extend the *Toolkit* Lesson

LANGUAGE PRACTICE
Similes

Read aloud books that use similes as a descriptive device, pausing when you encounter a simile to talk about it. Prompt children to infer what each simile means, and then check their interpretations with the illustrations in the book. *Quick Like a Cricket* by Audry Wood and Don Wood contains excellent examples of similes. Another resource is *Crazy Like a Fox: A Simile Story* by Loreen Leedy.

After reading aloud a few pages from one of these books, provide the students with pictures that they use to create their own descriptive similes. Kids glue a picture at the top of a page and use the frame for writing a simile:

_____ *like* _____, or _____ *as* _____. Model a couple of examples, and then they can try it.

Leaves hot like____Fire
The orange leaves red like____the sun.

Sparkling like_a disco ball
Cold____like__ice cream.

water falls like a faucet
flows like long hair.

Kids' similes for Language Practice.

CONTENT AND COMPREHENSION EXTENSION

Acting out verbs so that children understand more subtle differences between ways of moving provides an opportunity for kids to play with language as they speak and write their own poetry.

Display the following chart depicting ways to move. Divide the group into pairs and assign one of the movements—flying, jumping, crawling, or walking—to each pair. Kids work together to act out each word so their classmates can infer which word they are dramatizing.

fly	jump	crawl	walk
soar	hop	creep	slither
flutter	leap	wiggle	saunter
glide	bounce		pounce
swoop			

Follow up with an opportunity for kids to play with language to prepare to speak and write their own poetry. Using action pictures of people, animals, or other things and the verbs on the chart as starting points, show students how to build a simple list poem. For example:

Jaguar poem for Content and
Comprehension Extension.

Have students write and illustrate their own list poems. Collect them for a display or class poetry anthology.

LEARN to Visualize

Get
a picture
in your mind

PREVIEW GOALS

We want students to

CONTENT ▪ understand that poetry often has beautiful language that paints a picture in our minds.

COMPREHENSION ▪ understand that visualizing is a way to understand and interpret poetry.

LANGUAGE ▪ use different senses to create images in their minds, and then share those images through drawing, writing, and talking.

KEY VOCABULARY

COMPREHENSION WORDS
visualize
images

CONTENT WORDS
words related to the
poems to be read

LANGUAGE STRUCTURES

To prepare for the *Toolkit* lesson, the Preview teaches the language of visualizing.

I am visualizing _____.

The picture in my mind is _____.

Preview the *Toolkit* Lesson

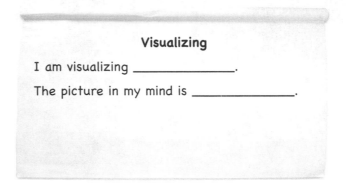

From *Honey, I Love and other love poems*, by Eloise Greenfield. Text copyright © 1978 by Eloise Greenfield. Used by permission of Harper Collins Publishers.

- To introduce the concept of visualizing, return to the poem "Butterfly" on page 48 of the *Keep Reading!* source book that you read in the Preview for Lesson 11. Read the poem aloud again, phrase by phrase, and ask kids what picture each phrase creates in their minds. Children use the visualizing sentence frame to describe what they see. For example: "I am visualizing a butterfly going from leaf to leaf."

Visualizing

I am visualizing _____.

The picture in my mind is _____.

- Kids sketch what they visualize for one of the phrases in the poem. Ask them to share their images with each other. They will discover that everyone creates a different picture in their minds and come to understand that we all have different interpretations of the words.

- For further practice, create a descriptive sentence (or read aloud one or more of the following examples). Ask students to draw what they visualize.

White, fluffy clouds float in the deep blue sky.

The raindrops felt like wet kisses on my face.

The trees were bending and swaying in the wind.

The snowflakes fell fast, creating a white blanket of snow.

Children's illustrations of descriptive language for the Preview.

Teach the *Toolkit* Lesson

Post the language structures charts from the Previews in both Lesson 12 (Inferring chart) and this lesson (Visualizing chart) to give the students access to the language that will help them begin to discuss their inferences and the pictures about the poems you read throughout the *Toolkit* lesson.

When the kids begin the Practice Independently section, confer with children to make sure they understand the vocabulary of the poem. Sketch pictures of the words if this helps to support word meaning. If they have difficulty with some of the words, it will be hard for them to visualize those words.

Extend the *Toolkit* Lesson

LANGUAGE PRACTICE
Metaphors

In this lesson, we introduce metaphors and how they can be used in poetry. Similes use the words *like* or *as*; metaphors are more direct.

The book *Skin Like Milk, Hair of Silk* by Brian Cleary has great examples of similes and metaphors and explains metaphors in a way kids can grasp. Cleary also has a great website with information about poetry and lots of language practice activities:

http://www.brianpcleary.com

Write a sentence containing metaphors on the board or a chart: *The blanket of snow warms the bed where the flowers lie sleeping.* Have kids turn and talk about the image that the words created in their minds. Then discuss the metaphors *blanket of snow* and *flowers lie sleeping*, asking, "What is the snow like?" (It is like a blanket.) "How does it act like a blanket?" (It keeps the flower bed warm.) "What are the flowers like?" (They are like people.) How are they like people? (They lie sleeping.) Then have them draw the image the words created in their minds. Kids can discuss and illustrate these metaphors:

Jessie is a math wizard.

Mamá stared at me with eyes of ice.

Her voice is music to my ears.

The crocodiles teeth are white daggers.

Child's illustration for Language Practice.

Or try these additional sentences, taken from poems in *Honey, I Love*.

My uncle's car is a parade float, carrying us into the country.

I am a "sweet little gingerbread girl."

Mama's a sweet, round plum dressed in her purple coat.

Listen to the angry mouse squeak of the piano pedal.

CONTENT AND COMPREHENSION EXTENSION

Kids love books by Dr. Seuss, and they often laugh out loud as they read them aloud. Seuss's work is funny and rhythmical and comes in many languages. Playing with poems written by him is fun for kids who are learning a new language simply because his poems are wild and wacky. As an extension, have kids choose part of a text written by Dr. Seuss and share it with a partner. Then help them prepare a shared read or an echo read to perform for the others. There is also a Dr. Seuss website that students can access to learn more about the author and his work:

http://www.seussville.com/Educators/educatorAuthor.php

MAKE SENSE of New Information

Infer from features, pictures, and words

PREVIEW GOALS

We want students to

CONTENT ▪ understand the concept of a life cycle.

COMPREHENSION ▪ infer to make sense of new information, particularly making a distinction between different visual features.

LANGUAGE ▪ learn signal words that describe a sequence of events, and practice how to talk about, draw, and record what they infer and visualize to facilitate learning from informational text.

KEY VOCABULARY

COMPREHENSION WORDS

first	second
sequence	third
then	fourth
next	

CONTENT WORDS

ladybug	stages
wings	egg
body	larva
head	pupa
antenna	adult
life cycle	

LANGUAGE STRUCTURES

To prepare students to talk about the life cycle of the ladybug in the *Toolkit* lesson text, the review provides practice with sequence words.

First, _____.
Next, _____.
Then, _____.
Finally, _____.

The first stage is _____.
The second stage is _____.
The third stage is _____.
The fourth stage is _____.

Preview the *Toolkit* Lesson

Used with permission from *TIME for Kids*.

- Preview vocabulary with the *TIME for Kids* poster titled "Ladybugs Grow Up," opening it up to its full poster size and reading and matching the labels to the images. Ask kids to turn and talk about what they know about ladybugs.

- Introduce the concept of a life cycle, and mention that the word *stages* means steps in the life cycle. Discuss each stage of the life cycle, following the numbers from 1 to 4 to explain how the ladybug grows from an egg into a larva, then becomes a pupa, and eventually grows into the insect that is the ladybug. Model the language structures that signal sequential thinking to help students understand the cycle. For example, "*First*, the ladybug lays the egg. *Then* we infer that the egg hatches and the larva is born. *Next*, the pupa is formed. We infer that the ladybug is growing inside the pupa. *Finally*, a ladybug is born."

Sequencing Language

First, _____.

Next, _____.

Then, _____.

Finally, _____.

The first stage is _____.

The second stage is _____.

The third stage is _____.

The fourth stage is _____.

- Understanding the sequence of the stages in the ladybug's life cycle will support students' inference making during the *Toolkit* lesson. Some children might choose to draw the ladybug life cycle.

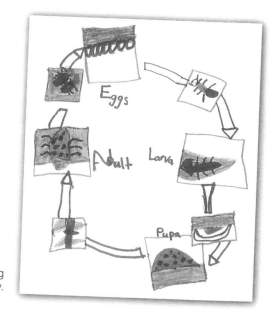

Drawing and labeling the ladybug life cycle during the Preview.

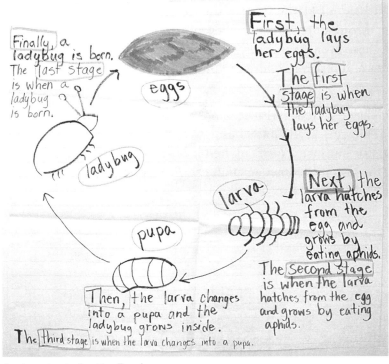

Stages of the Life Cycle of a Ladybug

Finally, a ladybug is born. The last stage is when a ladybug is born.

First, the ladybug lays her eggs. The first stage is when the ladybug lays her eggs.

eggs

ladybug

larva

pupa

Next, the larva hatches from the egg and grows by eating aphids. The second stage is when the larva hatches from the egg and grows by eating aphids.

Then, the larva changes into a pupa and the ladybug grows inside. The third stage is when the larva changes into a pupa.

Anchor charts for the Preview.

Teach the *Toolkit* Lesson

Post the language structures chart from the Preview. Before the *Toolkit* lesson begins, you might want to invite a student who participated in the Preview to introduce and provide background knowledge for the rest of the class about the "Ladybugs Grow Up" poster.

Extend the *Toolkit* Lesson

LANGUAGE PRACTICE
Sequencing

Extend the idea of sequence to familiar activities and events. Begin by asking kids to act out and name the steps of familiar actions, such as getting dressed to go outside by putting on hats, coats, mittens, and boots, or getting ready to ride a bike. Remember to post the signal words for students to use (*first*, *then*, and so on). Using the photographs on pages 100 and 101 and 118 and 119 of the Keep Reading! source book, students can talk through the sequence of events in these photographs. Kids can act out these event sequences. Another option is to copy and cut out the photos and text for children to put in order.

CONTENT AND COMPREHENSION EXTENSION

Locate photographs or sketches with accompanying text to describe different kinds of life cycles, and model using sequencing language to talk about them. For instance, "*First*, a kitten is born. *Then* the kitten grows up. *Next*, the kitten becomes an adult cat. *Finally*, the cat has its own kittens."

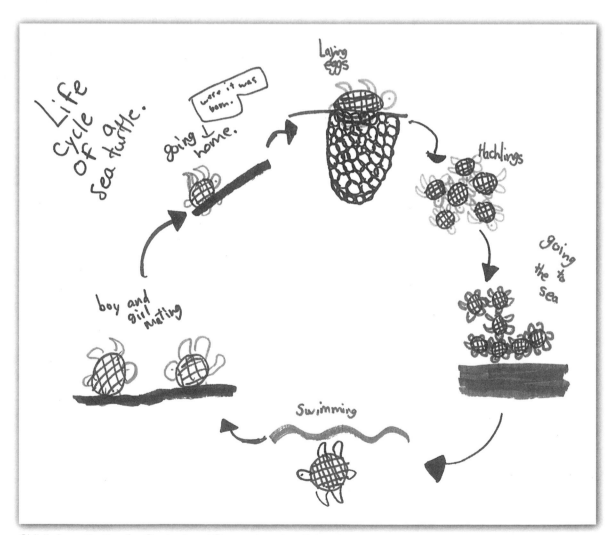

Child's investigation for Content and Comprehension Extension.

Next, mix a set of sequence word cards—*first, next, then, finally*—and images of the stages of that life cycle. Have children put the stages in order, place the word cards on top of the appropriate images, and then orally describe the cycle. An example of the life cycle from an egg to a chicken that could be cut up for children to put in order is on pages 50 and 51 of the Keep Reading! source book in *The Primary Comprehension Toolkit*

As children investigate the life cycles of living things, they can create their own informational posters or books that incorporate the idea of a sequence as well as visuals (photographs) and text features (labels and captions). As they are authoring their informational texts, encourage them to include their inferences about the information so they can share it with others. Making their thinking visible ("I think _____," "I learned _____") in this way adds voice and perspective to their writing.

Labeling pictures.

INFER and VISUALIZE with Narrative Nonfiction

Tie thinking to the text

PREVIEW GOALS

We want students to

CONTENT
- understand the relationship between animals and their habitats (in this case, Antarctica).

COMPREHENSION
- pay special attention to the illustrations, and build their inferences around information they gain from these pictures and text.

LANGUAGE
- distinguish between language that signals learning information (*I learned*) and language that denotes inferences (*I think*, *Maybe*, and *I infer*).

KEY VOCABULARY

COMPREHENSION WORDS
infer
ask questions
visualize
mind pictures

CONTENT WORDS
Antarctica
cold
freezing
windy
ice, icy
emperor penguin
leopard seal

LANGUAGE STRUCTURES

The Preview reviews language structures and frames that help kids talk about strategies that have already been taught—combining background knowledge with text clues from the story and pictures to make an inference.

I learned _____.
I wonder _____.
I think _____.
Maybe _____.
I infer _____.
I visualize _____.

Preview the *Toolkit* Lesson

Through drawing and writing about the Antarctic habitat, children learn new vocabulary and practice language structures as they talk about the habitat and animals.

- Page through *Antarctica* and identify the animals, also describing the habitat of Antarctica using vocabulary. Explain that the book takes place in Antarctica, which is at the South Pole—the farthest south you can go on Earth. Ascertain what children already know about the topic.

- Build a content landscape (a backdrop of a region) by quickly sketching a cold, icy, watery habitat, describing it using key vocabulary words like *cold*, *freezing*, *icy*, and *windy*. Have kids imagine what it feels like, acting out what it feels like to shiver in the cold or to walk against a howling wind.

- Label the landscape with content vocabulary, and use the language structures to talk about them.

Learning and Inferring

I learned _____.

I wonder _____.

I think _____.

Maybe _____.

I infer _____.

I visualize _____.

Content landscape for the Preview.

- Read the first few pages of *Antarctica*, prompting kids to share what they learn, infer, or visualize as they listen to the text and view the illustrations. Review the inferring equation from the previous lesson—explaining that we combine our background knowledge with the text clues, or the words and pictures in the text, to make inferences.

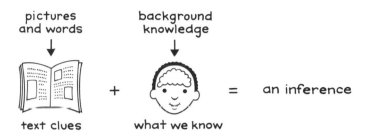

Emphasize that we infer from both the words and the pictures. Explain that as we listen to the words, we visualize, or create pictures in our minds of what is happening in the story.

Teach the *Toolkit* Lesson

Make the content landscape available for children to see and refer to so they can visualize the setting of the story during Connect and Engage. Post the language structures chart so they can participate during guided practice.

If children are more comfortable sketching a picture of their thinking instead of writing during the Collaborate time, confer briefly with kids and scribe their oral descriptions of their pictures and their inferences. This reinforces that inferring and visualizing are similar ways of thinking.

> **TOOLKIT GOALS**
>
> **We want students to**
> - combine their background knowledge with text and picture clues to draw inferences, make predictions, and visualize with narrative nonfiction.
> - draw inferences and create mind pictures in response to information, unfamiliar vocabulary, and the story.
> - infer big ideas and consider lingering question prompted by the text.

Extend the *Toolkit* Lesson

LANGUAGE PRACTICE
Contractions

Contractions can be tricky for students learning English as a new language and need to be explicitly taught and practiced. Begin by working with present tense contractions and the auxiliary verbs *be*, *can*, and *do*.

I am = I'm	they are = they're
it is = it's	cannot = can't
he is = he's	do not = don't
she is = she's	does not = doesn't
we are = we're	will not = won't

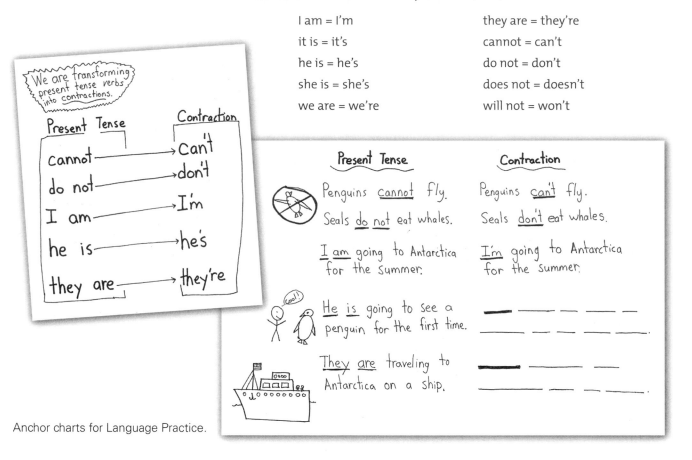

Anchor charts for Language Practice.

Create a poster or a thinksheet with verbs in their regular form (cannot) as well as contractions (can't). Provide a two-column chart with completed sample sentences and several examples left blank for students to fill in. Students write the sentences with the contracted form in the right column. Children practice reading and share their sentences with the group.

Read the original sentence	Rewrite the sentence with the contraction.
Penguins <u>cannot</u> fly.	Penguins can't fly.
In winter there <u>is not</u> a lot of light.	In winter there isn't a lot of light.
Female Emperor Penguins <u>do not</u> take care of their eggs.	Female emperor penguins don't take care of their eggs.
It is very cold in Antarctica.	It's very cold in Antarctica.

Thinksheet for Language Practice.

CONTENT AND COMPREHENSION EXTENSION

Antarctica and the *Toolkit* lesson both end with a lingering question: *Will people coming to Antarctica endanger the animals, or will the animals be able to survive?* Kids may want to investigate what is currently happening in this environment and the treaties and laws that have been enacted to protect it. This is a good opportunity to create maps and other visuals as well as text to demonstrate their learning.

Sources that are useful in answering this lingering question include *In Antarctica* by Marilyn Woolley, available at

http://www.myokapi.com

and an online site with information about how the environment and animals are protected by current treaties, available at

http://www.coolantarctica.com

Poster of information about Antarctica.

Thinking about lingering questions.

FIGURE OUT What's Important

Separate
important
information
from
interesting
details

PREVIEW GOALS

We want students to

CONTENT ▪ develop empathy for a person who overcame incredible obstacles in her life, so children understand the big ideas in the text.

COMPREHENSION ▪ make concrete the distinction between important information and interesting details.

LANGUAGE ▪ understand the concepts of being deaf, blind, and unable to speak, and use language that describes their feelings and emotions about these.

KEY VOCABULARY

COMPREHENSION WORDS
important information
details

CONTENT WORDS
blind
deaf
unable to speak
sign language
Braille

LANGUAGE STRUCTURES

To help students understand the nature of Helen Keller's disabilities, the Preview introduces language for expressing a personal response to Keller's challenges.

I felt _____.
    (I felt lonely.)

It made me feel _____.
    (It made me feel scared.)

It felt _____.
    (It felt sad.)

I couldn't _____.

Preview the *Toolkit* Lesson

■ Introduce key background concepts for the *TIME for Kids* (TFK) poster titled "Amazing Helen Keller": *blind, deaf, unable to speak.* Demonstrate and act these out so that kids understand each concept. Relate the descriptions of being blind to the sense of seeing; being deaf, to the sense of hearing.

■ Have the group act out and discuss these concepts, introducing the language structure stems *I felt _____* or *It made me feel _____*. Encourage kids to turn and talk as they try to imagine what it would feel like to be blind and deaf and to have difficulty speaking. Using the language structure stems, jot their feelings on an anchor chart.

Used with permission from *TIME for Kids.*

Feelings

I felt _____.

It made me feel _____.

It felt _____.

I couldn't _____.

■ To allow further elaboration, use the contraction *couldn't*. For example: *When my eyes were covered, I felt scared. It was dark. I <u>couldn't</u> see.*

■ Briefly preview and talk about the photographs in the TFK poster, discussing what kids notice. Explain that in the *Toolkit* lesson, we will put a star by the information we think is important as we read and view the poster. Draw a star on a Post-it, and put it next to the words: *She believed that blind and deaf people could do almost anything.* Emphasize that this is important information about Helen Keller that we want to remember. Now contrast this big idea with a detail, that she rode a horse, or wore old-fashioned clothing. Kids can chime in with details, too.

Teach the *Toolkit* Lesson

Post the Feelings language structures chart and the anchor chart containing children's responses to being blind, deaf, and unable to speak.

During collaborative practice, you may want to continue with a small version of the two-column ("Interesting Details"/"Important Information") chart rather than having students move immediately to starring important information. Guide students to write the facts they find on Post-its and then sort them, considering what they have written that is important information and what might be interesting details. When children have to sort their thinking in this way, they often have a clearer idea of the concepts.

TOOLKIT GOALS

We want students to

- recognize and understand what a detail is.
- distinguish important information from interesting details.
- code important information in the text with a star.

Extend the *Toolkit* Lesson

LANGUAGE PRACTICE
Adjectives

Using the senses to describe objects can give students practice with descriptive language as well as with syntax (how words are organized in a sentence).

Bring in a variety of objects. Make sure the objects can be easily described. Have students close their eyes, and hand them an object. Ask them to describe how the object feels or what sounds it makes. Jot down the vocabulary they use (for example, *soft, smooth, prickly, squeaky*). Then ask them to open their eyes, look at the object, and describe it again. Jot down the words they use (for example, *yellow, big, round*). Sketch a quick illustration to go along with the description of each object.

Once you have charted the adjectives students know, provide them with the language frame *The _____ _____ is _____.* Have them write about their object using two descriptive words based on what they see, feel, and hear (for example, *The yellow lemon is soft*). Be explicit about how word order (syntax) appears in English.

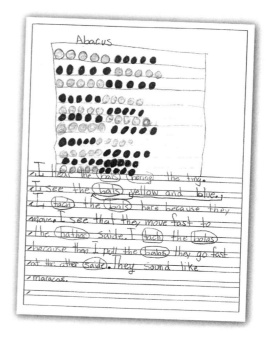

Child's response for Language Practice.

CONTENT AND COMPREHENSION EXTENSION

Kids are often fascinated by the sign language alphabet on the back of the "Amazing Helen Keller" poster. They enjoy using the sign language alphabet to spell out their names and send messages to one another.

Encourage those who are interested to investigate Braille. *The Black Book of Colors* by Menena Cottin and Rosana Faria aims to convey the experience of blindness to sighted readers. One kid-friendly site that explains the use of Braille, has an easily printed page of the Braille alphabet, and gives a biography of Helen Keller along with pictures is the Braille Bug website created by the American Foundation for the Blind:

http://www.afb.org/braillebug/

The website also explains more about how Helen Keller learned to speak and cultivate her remarkable talents. There is real footage of an interview with Helen Keller with her teacher Annie Sullivan, which can be accessed at

http://www.afb.org/braillebug/hkmuseum.asp

PARAPHRASE Information

Merge
your thinking
to make
meaning

PREVIEW GOALS

We want students to

CONTENT
- activate and use their content knowledge as a springboard for writing about a topic, in this case, Mexico.

COMPREHENSION
- merge their own thinking with information to learn and remember it.

LANGUAGE
- orally paraphrase information, extend their thinking about it, and then write and draw it.

KEY VOCABULARY

COMPREHENSION WORD
paraphrase

CONTENT WORDS
pyramid
festivals
holidays
Cinco de Mayo
dress up

LANGUAGE STRUCTURES

The Preview reviews the language frames for activating background knowledge and noticing new learning, and it introduces language frames for reporting information.

I see _____.
I notice _____.
I learned _____.
This reminds me of _____.
I know _____.
I think _____.

This is about _____.
What happens is _____.

Preview the *Toolkit* Lesson

In this Preview, we introduce the students to the idea of paraphrasing, and we practice with the *TIME for Kids* "A Visit to Mexico" poster that will be used in the *Toolkit* lesson. This gives kids a head start on what they will be asked to do during the whole-group lesson.

- Begin with the photos and images on the *TIME for Kids* poster titled "A Visit to Mexico," and have kids turn and talk about their background knowledge of the topic. Using Post-its, label some of the pictures so kids can connect the pictures with the written words.

- Using the children's information and comments, guide them to use the language frames as they talk about the information in their own words. The stems reinforce how kids merge their thinking with the information in the text.

Used with permission from *TIME for Kids*.

Noticing New Learning

I see _____.

I notice _____.

I learned _____.

This reminds me of _____.

I know _____.

I think _____.

This is about _____.

What happens is _____.

- Prepare the chart of directions for paraphrasing information you'll be using in the *Toolkit* lesson. Orally describe each step of the process. When you're done, ask kids to draw icons for each of these steps so they are familiar with them when they participate in the whole-group lesson.

Steps for Paraphrasing Information

- Read the information. Stop and think about it.

- Say the information in my own words, but don't say too much.

- React and respond to the information, merging my thinking with it.

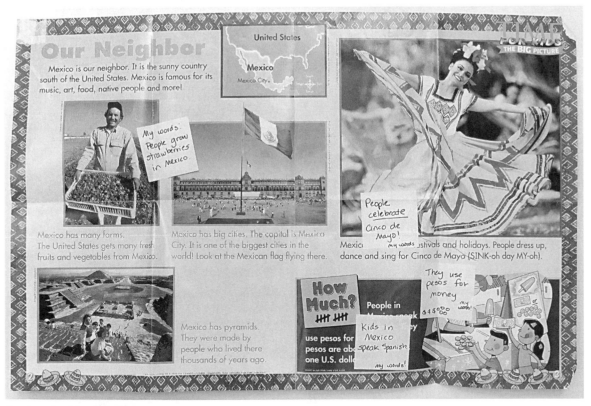

Anchor chart for Preview.

Teach the *Toolkit* Lesson

Rather than responding on Post-its during guided practice, it may be helpful for some children to respond on a color-coded Words from the Text/The Information in My Own Words thinksheet. Blue pens will help the kids underline the text they find interesting, while switching to a red pen signals for them that "these are my words."

As you confer with kids during the Collaborate and Practice

Independently sections, encourage them to talk with you or with one another about the image and the text before putting it in their own words. For some children, it may make sense to scribe their thoughts on a Post-it as they talk because kids often paraphrase without even thinking about it. Voiced writing allows us to put into print all the kids really know in their new language. We can also support them to use more elaborate language than they may be able to write on their own or introduce new vocabulary in a meaningful context.

Thinksheet for paraphrasing.

Extend the *Toolkit* Lesson

LANGUAGE PRACTICE
Phrasal Verbs

When we add a preposition or an adverb to a verb, its meaning may change. Kids need practice figuring out the meanings of phrases such as *dress up*, *catch up*, and *make up*.

Begin with the phrasal verb *dress up*, which is on the "A Visit to Mexico" poster: *This girl is dressed up for a festival.* Create a class chart that can be left up to guide kids to use these verbs. To make the phrasal verbs comprehensible, sketch a picture of several of these verbs as examples. Then show kids how to match the verb and the picture and act out the meaning. For instance, for *dress up*, we act out someone putting on a fancy outfit and talk through this as we do it.

Word	Meaning	Picture
dress up	dress in fancy clothes *I dress up for holidays.*	
catch up	hurry to be with *I ran to catch up with my friends.*	
warm up	get warm *I was freezing, so I put on my jacket to warm up.*	

Phrasal verbs for Language Practice.

Other expressions kids might work with include *eat out*, *look out*, *go out*, *back up*, *pop up*, and *clean up*. Once kids have been introduced to phrasal verbs, continue to refer to these and explain them when they come up in other texts or in conversations, adding the new expressions to the list.

CONTENT AND COMPREHENSION EXTENSION

Kids love to do research on a topic they select! Once kids understand how to put information in their own words, give them plenty of practice investigating, drawing, and writing about topics of their own choosing. Provide a rich variety of nonfiction at different reading levels from which kids can choose, and turn them loose.

To reinforce paraphrasing, guide children to read a text and then "put it in their own words" by drawing a picture and writing a brief caption about it. This is a great way to teach emergent readers and writers to put what they are learning into their own words.

If kids are interested in learning more about Mexico, check out several articles in *Toolkit Texts*, grades 2–3. "Celebrating the Day of the Dead," page 55, and "Mexico," pages 56–57, provide cultural and geographic information. Encourage kids to underline the information from the text in blue and to paraphrase the information in red next to the text.

ORGANIZE YOUR Thinking as You Read

Take notes to record information

PREVIEW GOALS

We want students to

CONTENT	▪ learn, wonder about, and respond to rain forest information.
COMPREHENSION	▪ take notes in their own words to learn and remember information.
LANGUAGE	▪ develop a line of thinking as they learn information, wonder about it, and respond to it.

KEY VOCABULARY

COMPREHENSION WORDS
fact
question
response

CONTENT WORDS
rain forest
blue frogs
toucan
sloth
canopy

LANGUAGE STRUCTURES

The Preview prepares kids for the *Toolkit* lesson's I learned/I wonder/Wow! anchor chart by reviewing language structures and stems used to identify information (facts), ask questions, and respond to information.

	What is it?	What do we say?
Facts	state information we learn	I learned _____.
Questions	ask or wonder about information	I wonder _____.
		How _____?
		Why _____?
		Where _____?
		When _____?
		What _____?
		Who _____?
Responses	react to information, connect to it express thoughts, feelings, or opinions	Wow! I'm amazed _____. I'm surprised _____.

Preview the *Toolkit* Lesson

Used with permission from *TIME for Kids*.

The Preview introduces children to rain forest animals they will read about on the *TIME for Kids* poster "Welcome to the Rain Forest." Children are familiar with ways to talk about facts (*I learned*) and questions (*I wonder* and the question words); now we introduce language stems for reacting and responding to information.

- Preview the *TIME for Kids* "Welcome to the Rain Forest" poster, encouraging kids' excitement about the amazing creatures. Ascertain their background knowledge about the rain forest.

- Show the photos and read the captions on page 2. Model the response frames on the anchor chart as you encounter new information. For example: "<u>I'm amazed!</u> Poisonous frogs are blue!" Explain that there are lots of ways to show excitement about new information, introducing the response frames "I'm amazed _____, I'm surprised _____, and Wow!"

I learned, I wonder, Wow!

	What is it?	**What do we say?**
Facts	state information we learn	I learned _____.
Questions	ask or wonder about information	I wonder _____.
		How _____.?
		Why _____.?
		Where _____.?
		When _____.?
		What _____.?
		Who _____.?
Responses	react to information, connect to it	Wow!
		I'm amazed _____.
	express thoughts, feelings, or opinions	I'm surprised _____.

- Now model what you wonder, using a question or two: "Why are they such bright colors?" "How are they poisonous?" "Are they poisonous if you touch them?" Encourage children to use these language frames and their own drawing to respond as you read aloud.

Child's response to the rain forest poster during Preview.

- Show kids the chart—with three columns titled "I learned," "I wonder," and "Wow!"—that they will be working with during the *Toolkit* lesson, and review the thinking and language for each column.

I learned	I wonder	Wow!

Teach the *Toolkit* Lesson

To begin the *Toolkit* lesson, ask children who participated in the Preview to act as rain forest specialists and share some things they already have learned or take their classmates on a tour of the website kids have already visited. Either way of sharing and introducing the topic to others builds children's confidence as "teachers" and provides them with important practice speaking in front of a group about familiar information.

> ## TOOLKIT GOALS
>
> **We want students to**
> - react and respond as they read and learn information.
> - distinguish between—and record—facts, questions, and responses to keep track of their thinking.
> - sort and organize thinking on the *I learned/I wonder/Wow!* anchor chart and thinksheet.

Color-coding kids' responses helps them to distinguish between facts, questions, and responses. When conferring or working with a small group during Collaborate or Practice Independently, model how to write what they learn in one color, their questions in another color, and their responses in a third color.

Extend the *Toolkit* Lesson

LANGUAGE PRACTICE
Interjections

Interjections, or exclamations, allow children to express surprise, delight, and excitement as they learn new information. Demonstrate the tone used with these expressions, and contrast it with the tone used for simple statements.

Using text and photos in books or other sources, ask students to practice turning and talking about amazing information they encounter as they read or view photographs. Support them to use the following frames:

Wow!	Amazing!	Oh, no!	I never knew!
Cool!	Huh?!	Whoa!	How interesting!

Show kids how to elaborate on their interjections with information that tells what amazed them.

Frame: Wow! _____!

Frame with response: Wow! Sloths can hang upside down for hours!

Share out and post the kids' thinking and images along with their exclamations on a chart or on the class rain forest mural.

wow! That coolthat sloths move so slowly.

coolIt never knew there we're black jaguars.

Children's responses from Language Practice.

CONTENT AND COMPREHENSION EXTENSION

Encourage kids to explore and investigate rain forest animals or any other topic they are interested in and to take notes using the *I learned/ I wonder/Wow!* anchor chart note-taking scaffold.

Check out the website with an interactive rain forest at night (mentioned in the Preview) where kids can click on animals that live in the different layers of the rain forest:

http://www.nationalgeographic.com/features/00/earthpulse/rainforest/index_
   flash-feature.html

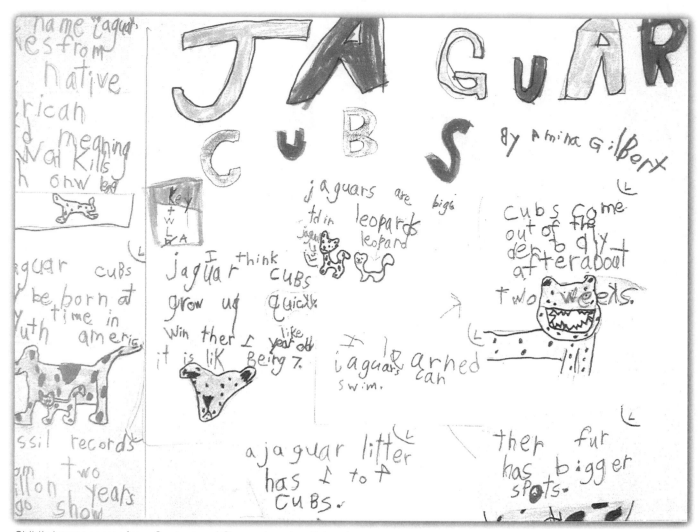

Child's jaguar poster from Content and Comprehension Extension.

SUMMARIZE Information

Put it in your own words and keep it interesting

PREVIEW GOALS

We want students to

CONTENT ■ shape rain forest information into their own thought as a summary.

COMPREHENSION ■ understand that a summary is about saying the information in your own words and not telling too much.

LANGUAGE ■ use phrases that state or report new learning.

KEY VOCABULARY

COMPREHENSION WORDS
summary
summarize

CONTENT WORDS
rain forest
blue frogs
toucan
sloth
canopy

LANGUAGE STRUCTURES

To launch the new strategy, Summarize and Synthesize, the Preview teaches the language of summarizing.

This was mostly about _____.

I learned _____.

I also learned _____.

I was amazed to learn _____.

The most interesting things I learned were _____ and _____.

Preview the *Toolkit* Lesson

Have kids practice putting information into a summary frame during this Preview.

Return to the "Welcome to the Rain Forest" poster, and focus on one of the photographs and captions on pages 2 and 3. To review how to learn information from photographs and the text, model how kids can view the photograph and read the words to learn information.

■ Read the information and demonstrate how to use one of the language frames to talk about the information ("I was amazed to learn that the frog's bright blue color tells other animals to stay away!"). Ask kids to turn and talk with each other about something they learned using the language frames.

Used with permission from *TIME for Kids*.

Summarizing

This was mostly about _____.

I learned _____.

I also learned _____.

I was amazed to learn _____.

The most interesting things I learned were
_____ and _____.

■ Preview with the children the chart titled "How to Create a Summary" from *Toolkit* Lesson 19. Explain that when we summarize, we tell what something is about in just a few words. Talk about each step, and add sketches to help children remember what each step is.

How to Create a Summary

1. Reread your notes on the topic. Make sure they are accurate and in your own words.

2. Think about the topic and the information that tells about it.

3. Put the notes in order—what comes first, second, third.

4. Remember to tell what is important, but don't tell too much.

Children's responses from the Preview.

Teach the *Toolkit* Lesson

Post the chart titled "How to Create a Summary" along with sketches to remind children of the procedure during guided practice.

When the students are working independently, support them by helping them read each other's Post-its. Share possibilities for the first sentence to get them started. For students who may be reticent to write, engage them in a conversation about what they know and have learned, and scribe what they say on the Post-its. Then they can organize the information into a summary by themselves.

Extend the *Toolkit* Lesson

LANGUAGE PRACTICE
Idioms

Common idioms are abstract, so we need to explicitly teach them. Kids love to act out idioms and drawing both their literal and figurative meanings helps kids make sense of them.

Using two columns, write the idiom and ask the kids to help sketch its literal meaning in the first two columns. Guide discussion about the idiomatic meaning, and then sketch the intended meaning of the idiom and describe what it means in the third column.

Idiom	Picture (what the words say)	Picture and Words (what they really mean)

Rise and shine!

Get up in the morning ready to go!

Anchor chart of idioms for Language Practice.

CONTENT AND COMPREHENSION EXTENSION

One of the best ways to practice paraphrasing and summarizing is for kids to draw animals and write captions about them. For reference, see the "Content Literacy: Reading, Writing, and Research" video on the DVD in *The Primary Comprehension Toolkit*, which illustrates how first graders summarize the information they have learned and add it to their "living example" of the rain forest. This is an easily differentiated activity. Children who draw a picture or cut out an animal can use anything from a short caption to a full paragraph to describe their animal. See the language frames for writing a summary.

Language frames for writing a summary during Content and Comprehension Extension.

> **How to Write a Summary**
>
> I read _____.
> I learned _____.
> I also learned _____.
> Another thing I learned was _____.
> The most interesting thing I learned was _____.

For an additional source of information and images, check out

http://www.nationalgeographic.com/features/00/earthpulse/rainforest/index_
    flash-feature.html

I learned

boas can climb trees to the canopy layer.

canopy layer

WOW That is AMAZING

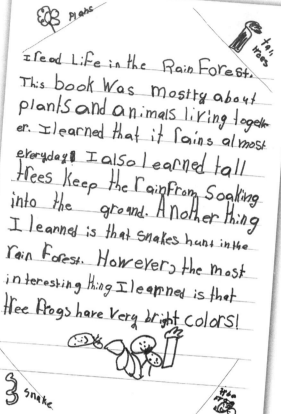

plants

tall trees

I read Life in the Rain Forest. This book was mostly about plants and animals living together. I learned that it rains almost everyday! I also learned tall trees keep the rain from soaking into the ground. Another thing I learned is that snakes hunt in the rain forest. However, the most interesting thing I learned is that tree frogs have very bright colors!

snake

tree frog

Children's summaries—Content and Comprehension Extension.

READ TO Get the Big Ideas

Synthesize
the text

PREVIEW GOALS

We want students to

CONTENT ▪ understand the rain forest habitat, how animals are adapted to it, and what is happening as rain forest habitat disappears.

COMPREHENSION ▪ use information to infer and arrive at big ideas about the rain forest habitat.

LANGUAGE ▪ infer the meaning of descriptive and sensory language, and use this language themselves.

KEY VOCABULARY

COMPREHENSION WORDS
big ideas
infer

CONTENT WORDS
kapok tree
tree frog
anteater
tree porcupines or sloths
jaguar
macaw
monkey
bee
boa constrictor

LANGUAGE STRUCTURES

Descriptive language can seem abstract for new speakers of a language. In the Preview, we demonstrate how kids can use their senses to help them interpret the descriptive language and events in the *Toolkit* lesson text, *The Great Kapok Tree*.

It looks like _____.
It feels like _____.
It sounds like _____.
It tastes like _____.
It smells like _____.

I see _____.
I feel _____.
I hear _____.
I taste _____.
I smell _____.

Preview the *Toolkit* Lesson

From *The Great Kapok Tree* by Lynne Cherry. Copyright © 1990. Reprinted by permission of Harcourt, Inc.

Children are introduced to some of the animals living around or in the great kapok tree in the *Toolkit* lesson text. The rich sensory language brings the reader into the rain forest scene, so ask kids to "step into the story" and imagine being there so they can experience it in a concrete way.

- Read and discuss the illustrations and text on the first few pages of *The Great Kapok Tree*, looking at the pictures and discussing the sensory language that describes the rain forest.

- On the first page, model how the forest was "alive with the sounds of squawking birds and howling monkeys." Let kids turn and talk and make these sounds, adding others they think they might hear in a rain forest. Then dramatize how the forest becomes quiet and silent when the two men enter and point to the tree.

- On the next page, read paragraph 1. Ask kids to imagine they are in the story and to act out the part when the man begins to chop the tree down. Discuss that the man grew tired in the hot, steamy forest. Kids use the language structures to describe what the man is experiencing.

> <u>I hear</u> buzzing and chirping insects.
>
> <u>I feel</u> hot and sleepy.
>
> <u>I see</u> huge trees and plants dripping with raindrops.

Using Senses to Describe

It looks like _____.

It feels like _____.

It sounds like _____.

It tastes like _____.

It smells like _____.

I see _____.

I feel _____.

I hear _____.

I taste _____.

I smell _____.

Anchor chart from the rain forest Preview.

■ To guide kids to infer and put words that the animals "say" into their own words, read on and ask kids again to "step into the story" and "become" the animals. As kids take on the roles of the characters, show them how to put the words of the green tree boa in their own words. Read the text. Discuss the meaning of the words. Have a child act out the role of the animal, and model how to paraphrase the text in simpler, clearer language that captures the big idea. Following are some examples.

Boa constrictor
Words from the text: *"This is a tree of miracles. It is my home, where generations of my ancestors have lived. Do not chop it down."*

Paraphrase: *I am the green tree boa! This tree is amazing! It is my home! Please do not cut it down!*

Child's response to
The Great Kapok Tree.

Bee

Words from the text: *"My hive is in this Kapok tree, and I fly from tree to tree and flower to flower collecting pollen. In this way I pollinate the trees and flowers throughout the rain forest. You see, all living things depend on one another."*

Paraphrase: *I am the bee! I help the plants grow. They would not grow without me! All living things need each other, so please do not cut down the tree.*

Teach the *Toolkit* Lesson

Kids who participated in the Preview might act out how the animals "spoke" to the sleeping man, illustrating how they put the language of the story into their own words and sharing this with the whole class.

Language structures can be posted to support kids to write and draw sensory images as they respond to the story during the read-aloud.

Extend the *Toolkit* Lesson

Prepare captions that describe the actions and sounds of the animals in the story, but add some blanks so that kids can figure out which animal did each action. Since kids have heard the story, read a few of the captions together and see if kids can figure out which animal matches the appropriate action or sound. Encourage them to act out the actions and sounds as they figure out which animal they are, building on the sensory language introduced during the Preview. After a few examples, kids work with a partner to read their caption, act out the animal, and challenge the rest of the group to guess who they are and what they are doing.

The _____ slithered.
The boa constrictor slithered.

The _____ slid close to the man.
The huge snake slid close to the man.

The _____ hissed.
The snake hissed loudly—sssssssssssss!

A bee buzzed.

A troupe of monkeys scampered.
The monkeys chattered.

A toucan flew.
A toucan squawked.

A tree frog crawled.
The tree frog squeaked.

A jaguar leaped down from the tree and padded silently toward the man.

The tree porcupine swung down from his branch and whispered to the man.

CONTENT AND COMPREHENSION EXTENSION

In preparation for Lesson 22, in which kids choose a project—mural, poster, book, or poem—that reflects their learning, guide them to create poems using sensory words. Draw on the information the kids have learned as rain forest researchers to put all their thinking together and write about it in creative ways.

Begin by brainstorming descriptive words and phrases connected to the rain forest or another topic being studied.

What We Hear

Bees are buzzing—
BZZZZZZZ!

Ssssssss—snakes
are hissing!

Monkeys are chattering.

Toucans and macaws
are squawking.

How It Feels

hot and wet

What We See

Raindrops drip from leaves.

Monkeys swing through
the trees.

Toucans throw fruit in the air
and catch it in their beaks.

Butterflies flit from flower
to flower.

Students work in small groups to create a poem using descriptive language. Choose any rain forest animal or one of the layers of the rain forest habitat that the kids know a lot about. Have kids turn and talk together, asking each child to come up with one phrase about the topic. Kids share their phrases. Jot them on a chart, and help children to reorganize the phrases into a poem. When the poem is done, kids use the words to create visual images and illustrate the poem.

Rain forest poetry
for the Content and
Comprehension Extension.

EXPLORE and Investigate

Read, write, and draw in a researcher's workshop

PREVIEW GOALS

We want students to

CONTENT ▪ summarize and synthesize information and new learning.

COMPREHENSION ▪ understand how to express information clearly—through drawing and writing—to take thinking public.

LANGUAGE ▪ share information with voice, confidence, and enthusiasm.

KEY VOCABULARY

COMPREHENSION WORDS
synthesize
research
poster
words for visual and
  text features

CONTENT WORDS
words from previous
  lessons on the rain forest

LANGUAGE STRUCTURES

The Preview reviews interjections and the language of new learning so that kids can communicate their enthusiasm for the research topics they will be identifying during the *Toolkit* lesson.

I never knew _____.
Amazing! I learned _____.
Can you believe _____?

Preview the *Toolkit* Lesson

The purpose of *Toolkit* Lesson 21 is to spur kids on to use all the *Toolkit* strategies to do research—read, write, draw, organize, and share information on a topic they are investigating. This isn't simply a one-shot lesson; instead, the goal is to make researching become a way of life in classrooms where kids eagerly do research independently!

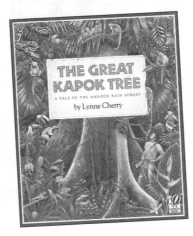 

From *The Great Kapok Tree* by Lynne Cherry. Copyright © 1990. Reprinted by permission of Harcourt, Inc. Used with permission from *TIME for Kids*.

To prepare kids to do research on their own, we collaborate and begin to create a poster together, showing them the process of how to write and illustrate the information they know on a poster.

- Help kids select an animal that they already know a lot about. They turn and talk, using the language structures to share what information they found most interesting about the topic.

Expressing Amazement

I never knew _____.

Amazing! I learned _____.

Can you believe _____?

- Sketch the animal on a chart, and ask kids to turn and talk about what they know about it. As kids come up with information, ask them to write it on Post-its or sentence strips and add these to the poster.

- Prompt kids to think about anything they still wonder about, noting that research posters often include questions. Jot these on the chart.

Kids create posters to share their new learning.

In the poster:

I think Toucans T
throw the fruit in
the air and catch
it.

A Toucans eat
oo c t>ov fruit
→all kinds of

I learned Toucans ?
eat fruit? I wonder
what kind of
fruit?
I think they
eat

No, I dont think
they can fly.
- Because I have
a lot of different
reasons
- They have a
big beak-
I don't they can
carry it.

I learned the L
toucan lives in
the canopy.
I wonder if
the toucan can
fly

- Ask kids to think about illustrations and features that would teach others about their animal. Some kids might suggest a close up of a body part, or labeling the parts of the animal. Kids contribute a visual or text feature to the poster—and often they come up with original and creative features to share information.

- Wrap up the session by explaining that when we create a poster like this, we are synthesizing information, or putting together all we know to teach this to others.

Teach the *Toolkit* Lesson

If one or two kids are enthusiastic about the animal model from the Preview session, encourage these kids to continue to work on this poster.

The experience of beginning to create a research poster supports kids to try one on their own during the Collaborate and Practice Independently portions of the lesson.

TOOLKIT GOALS

We want students to

- use comprehension strategies as tools for research and investigation.
- independently read for information, ask and answer questions, and record new learning.
- begin to synthesize information on a poster.

Extend the *Toolkit* Lesson

LANGUAGE PRACTICE
Sharing

Giving new learners of English explicit language for sharing their work and learning supports them to feel confident during sharing time.

Develop a how-to poster about what researchers do when they share.

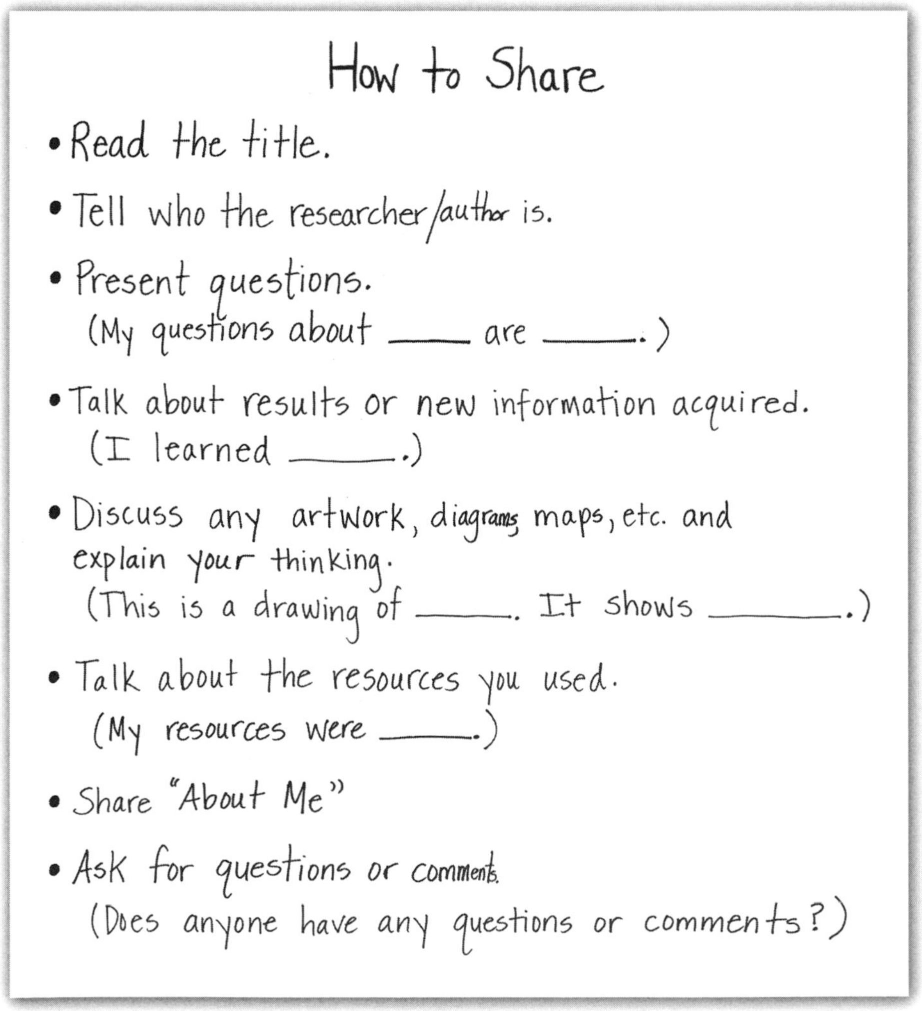

How to Share
• Read the title.
• Tell who the researcher/author is.
• Present questions.
(My questions about ____ are ____.)
• Talk about results or new information acquired.
(I learned ____.)
• Discuss any artwork, diagrams, maps, etc. and explain your thinking.
(This is a drawing of ____. It shows ____.)
• Talk about the resources you used.
(My resources were ____.)
• Share "About Me"
• Ask for questions or comments.
(Does anyone have any questions or comments?)

Poster for Language Practice.

To reinforce the procedures for asking questions, finding new information, and engaging in the research process, create a mind map that shows the process. Include the different kinds of resources kids use to investigate their topics, examples of different kinds of projects, and samples of ways to draw and represent thinking. Creating a mind map consolidates all our thinking about the process in an engaging visual artifact that guides kids as they continue to engage in research and investigation.

Begin with a central theme (like rain forest) and symbolic illustrations to represent it. Then branch out clockwise adding drawings, text, and colors to represent and explain our learning.

Mind map of rain forest learning for Content and Comprehension Extension.

Kids share the results of their explorations

SHARE YOUR Learning

Create projects to demonstrate understanding

PREVIEW GOALS

We want students to

CONTENT
- understand different ways of synthesizing content information—posters, poems, books, art.

COMPREHENSION
- understand what it means to comment on and respond to someone else's work and thinking.
- gain a sense of teaching what they know to others, including peers and teachers.

LANGUAGE
- use and understand language for sharing their work and discussing it with others as well as respond to other children's work.

KEY VOCABULARY

COMPREHENSION WORDS
poster
poem
self-published book
synthesize

CONTENT WORDS
words appropriate for
 the topic

LANGUAGE STRUCTURES

During the Preview, we review a routine for sharing and discussing learning as they present to one another and a variety of language stems for responding.

Researcher (says when presentation is done): What questions, comments, or connections do you have?

Responder:
 I like the way you _____.
 I love your research because _____.
 I have a question. I'm wondering about _____.
 I have a connection. I'm thinking _____. *or* It reminds me of _____.

Researcher (calls on another volunteer): _____, would you like to share?

Preview the *Toolkit* Lesson

In this Preview, kids rehearse both the language they will use as they share their own work and the way they will respond as an audience.

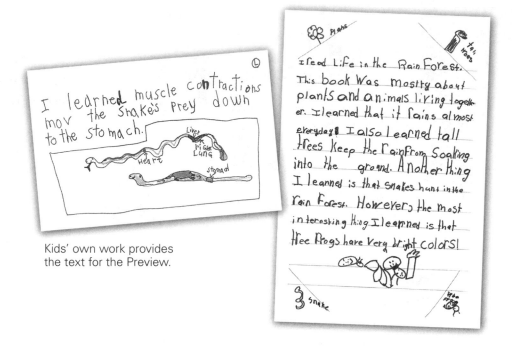

Kids' own work provides the text for the Preview.

- Ask one child to share a piece of work of his or her own: the poem from the Content and Comprehension Extension in Lesson 20, a contribution to the group rain forest poster in Lesson 21, or any other project. (See the Language Practice activity in Lesson 21; post the What Researchers Do When They Share how-to chart to guide kids.) Explain to the kids that together you will talk about the child's project, responding and commenting on the work.

- Teach kids the researcher-responder language stems that they can use to initiate responses to their work.

Responding to Research

Researcher: What questions, comments, or connections do you have?

Responder:
  I like the way you _____.
  I love your research because _____.
  I have a question. I'm wondering about _____.
  I have a connection. I'm thinking _____. or
     It reminds me of _____.

Researcher: _____, would you like to share?

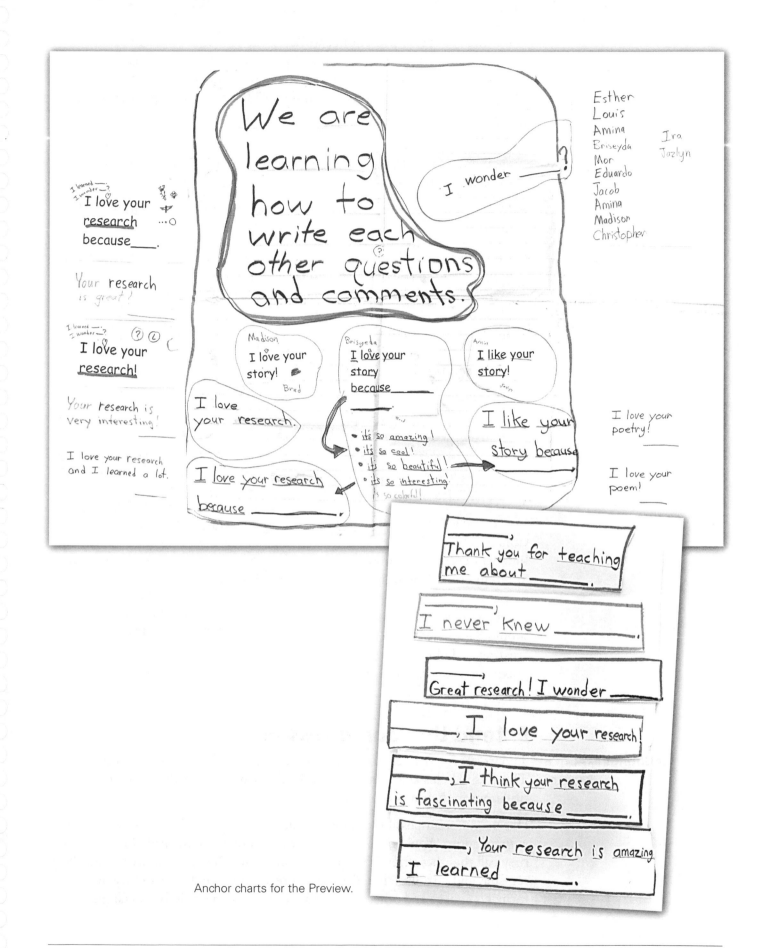

Anchor charts for the Preview.

- Let the researcher present her work. At the end of the presentation, prompt her to initiate discussion: "What comments, questions, or connections do you have?" Have her call on someone respectfully: "_____, would you like to share?" Prompt the responder to answer: "Yes, thank you," before continuing.

- Review the responding stems on the language structures chart, and encourage the presenter to call on several kids so all can practice using the stems to respond.

- Kids write or draw their responses on Post-its and add these to the presenter's work.

- End by showing kids the options for sharing learning—posters, poems, books, etc.—so that kids are familiar with the vocabulary that describes each when they choose a project during the *Toolkit* lesson. Have a sample of each project (or the mind map created for the Lesson 21 Content and Comprehension Extension) available for kids to look at. Explain that when we create a project we are synthesizing, or putting together, all the information we have learned.

Teach the *Toolkit* Lesson

Refer to the chart of options for sharing learning if kids have not yet decided on a project.

Conferences during the Collaborate and Practice Independently times allow for differentiation. Children who participated in the Language Practice session in Lesson 20 should have a head start on creating and illustrating a poem about the rain forest.

> **TOOLKIT GOALS**
>
> **We want students to**
> - summarize and synthesize what they learn by making posters, poems, books, and other projects.
> - share new knowledge and teach it to their peers and teachers.
> - participate in a community of researchers by thoughtfully responding to each other's projects.

Extend the *Toolkit* Lesson

LANGUAGE PRACTICE
Register

The word *register* refers to the way we talk in formal and casual conversations. This lesson helps kids be alert to the kind of language they're using in different situations in their new language.

Discuss different possibilities for the language they could use with friends or with an adult. Would they say "dude" while addressing the principal? Would they call their best friend "sir" or "ma'am"? Take the opportunity to talk about register, and introduce the idea that there are times and places to use more formal language and other times and places to use more informal language.

Ask kids to role-play these situations with a partner.

Situation	Casual	Formal
playing at recess	playing tag with your friends	telling the principal what happened
eating lunch	eating with your friends	ordering in a restaurant
saying "hello"	to your little sister	to your grandmother

CONTENT AND COMPREHENSION EXTENSION

This is the perfect opportunity to continue to build students' knowledge about an important ecosystem and reinforce the big idea that this habitat is disappearing at record rates for many reasons. Essential questions such as, *What is happening to the rain forest habitats?* and *Why are rain forests disappearing?* provide opportunities for kids to engage with issues and with people who are trying to save these delicate habitats.

Anchor chart about taking action—Content and Comprehension Extension.

Kids can learn more and take action using the suggestions on the Rain Forest Action Network's website at

http://ran.org/content/get-involved

They can find a map of rain forests at

http://www.blueplanetbiomes.org/rainforest.htm

Preparing a Post-it to share.

Appendices

Lesson 1: **Think About the Text** *(page 1)*

TEACHING MOVES	TEACHING LANGUAGE
▪ **Preview the book by doing a picture walk or briefly telling the beginning of the story. Explain that when we read, listen, and view, we are thinking.**	We have thoughts of our own when we look at the pictures and listen to or read a book. We think about the story and our own ideas as we read and this helps us understand it!
▪ **Demonstrate how to think about the text.**	I'm going to show you how I think about the words and pictures.
	We might be reminded of something that's happened to us, so we can say, "This reminds me of _____."
	This story makes me think about _____. So we could say, " I think _____."
	Or you can tie your thinking to what is happening in the story and say, "When _____, it reminded me of _____."
▪ **Ask kids to turn and talk about something the text reminds them of or makes them think about, using the frames. Listen in and prompt as needed.**	Now it's your turn. What does this make you think about? What does it remind you of?
	Remember to use our language frames: I think _____. This reminds me of _____. This makes me think about _____.
▪ **Explain that when we read, listen, and view, we can leave tracks of our thinking by writing and drawing. Model how you leave tracks of your thinking**	When we write and draw our thinking, we say we are leaving tracks of our thinking, like tracks in the snow or the sand! Now watch me as I write and draw my thinking.
▪ **Invite the kids to write or draw what the text makes them think about.**	Now you try writing and drawing what you are thinking about.

Lesson 2: **Notice and Think About Nonfiction Features** *(page 7)*

TEACHING MOVES

- **Locate and label different features using the language frame, I see _____ .**

- **Give kids Post-its with the names of each feature so they can match it to the features they find in the text.**

- **Explain the word purpose.**

- **Describe some purposes.**

- **Model language frames used to describe the purpose of a feature. Ask kids to name a feature, explain its purpose, and share what it tells them.**

- **Model how we learn information from features.**

- **Invite kids to turn and talk about what they learn from features.**

TEACHING LANGUAGE

Nonfiction is full of special features.
Here are some of them.
I see a photograph.
I see a caption.
I see bold print.

Let's use these Post-its to label each feature. We can put the name of each feature next to it.

Writers and illustrators include features for a reason or a purpose. They help us understand the information better.

Here are some of the ways different features help us learn information.
A photograph shows us what something looks like.

A caption gives us information about photographs or illustrations.

Bold print tells us to pay attention.

Let's talk about some of these purposes. I can say:
I see a _____. This feature tells me that _____.

We can learn a lot of information from features!
From the _____, I learned _____. As I looked carefully at the _____, I learned that _____.

Now it's your turn. Look carefully at the different features, and then turn and talk with a partner about something you learned from them.

Lesson 3: **Explore Nonfiction Features** *(page 13)*

TEACHING MOVES

- **Explain that we are going to describe features and what they teach us.**

- **Model the language structure used to identify and describe features.**

- **Model drawing a feature and then adding labels or captions.**

- **Ask kids to try this.**

TEACHING LANGUAGE

We are going to review different features and talk about what they tell us, teach us, and show us.

Let's review the features and their purposes.
This is a _____. It tells me _____.
This is a _____. It teaches me _____.
This is a _____. It shows _____.

I'm drawing a _____ (feature) and writing a _____ (feature). It is teaching/showing us that _____.

Go ahead and draw and write features about something you know a lot about.
To share your information, you can say This is a _____. It _____.
Be sure to add labels or captions to your feature and talk about what it shows or teaches us.

TEACHING MOVES	TEACHING LANGUAGE
■ **Explain to kids that they will be writing about things they know and are passionate about. Explain what a specialist is and what it means to have a passion.**	Every person here is a specialist. A specialist is someone who knows a lot about something and cares about it.
■ **Invite kids to talk to each other about their specialties.**	You are all specialists. Who loves animals? Who likes to play a sport? Turn and talk about your specialty.
■ **Model language structures for talking and writing about specialist topics.**	When we talk and write about what we are specialist in, we can say: I know _____. I know a lot about _____. I learned _____. I like _____. I love _____. Did you know _____?
■ **Explain conversational moves for talking about their specialist topics.**	As you turn and talk with someone about your topic, you can ask your friend, "What do you know a lot about? What do you care about?"
■ **Bring kids back together to create a list of the topics they are interested in writing about.**	It's your turn to tell us about things you know a lot about and care about. When we share out our ideas, we get more ideas for what we can write about and teach others!

Lesson 5: **Think About What You Know** *(page 21)*

TEACHING MOVES

- **Explain to the kids that they are going to talk about what they will write in their specialist books.**

- **Model how to write and draw about your topic, perhaps drawing a picture and writing a caption, talking about what you do as you do it.**

- **Ask kids to try drawing and writing something about their topic, making sure to describe their topic or teach others something interesting about it.**

- **Share out kids' drawing and writing as this gives children ideas for their own teaching books.**

TEACHING LANGUAGE

I'm going to write and illustrate my teaching book about _____. My teaching book is nonfiction. Remember that when we read nonfiction, we learn new information.

I'm going to use some features like labels and captions to tell about my topic, which is _____.

Notice how I'm drawing a picture and writing about it. I'm using _____ and _____ (labels and captions or other features).

Now you try it. Remember what I did:
I described what I know about _____ and wrote it down.
I drew features, such as a picture that shows my thinking or what I know.
I thought about what I wanted to teach you about _____ and made sure I included that!

Remember to use these frames to talk about your topic.
I know _____.
I learned _____.
I like to _____.
I like _____ because _____.
I love _____ because _____.

Let's share out some of your ideas. In this way, we can learn so much from each other!

Lesson 6: **Make Connections** *(page 25)*

- **Explain the idea of inner voice.**

- **As you show kids the first few pages of the book, model your inner voice is what saying and your connection.**

- **Link the strategy of making connections to the language structures.**

- **Explain that when we make a connection, we understand the story better because we are relating to our own lives and experiences. Suggest some language frames that show how a connection helps you understand the story.**

When we look at pictures, listen, or read, we have a voice in our head that speaks to us. We call that our inner voice. It is the thinking we do when we listen and read.

As I look at the pictures or read the words, I hear my inner voice saying _____. I have a connection. That means something in the story reminds me of something that happened to me.

So here is how I would say I have a connection.
This reminds me of _____.
I have a connection _____.
I have a connection because _____.
My connection is ___. This helps me understand because _____.

You might say,
I think I know how _____ feels because when I _____, I felt _____.

When this happened to me, I _____.

I felt like _____ because _____.

When we make connections between the story and our experiences, we understand the story better!

Lesson 7: **Merge Thinking with New Learning** *(page 29)*

(page 29)

TEACHING MOVES	TEACHING LANGUAGE
■ **Explain that when we read nonfiction, we think about what we already know about a topic.**	When we read nonfiction, we think about our background knowledge. Your background knowledge is what you already know about _____.
■ **Model how we think about our background knowledge as we read, listen, and view.**	Look at this photograph of a _____. I already know about _____. I know _____. That's my background knowledge!
■ **Model how we can learn new information as we read, listen, or view.**	When I looked at this photo and read this text, I learned that _____.
■ **Ask kids to try it.**	Go ahead and turn and talk about your background knowledge about _____ or what you learned about _____.
■ **Show kids how you stop, think, and react to new information.**	When I see _____ or notice _____, I'm thinking, Wow! _____. I didn't know _____. Amazing _____. It's amazing that _____. I never knew that _____. These are my reactions or responses to the information. Now you try it. Remember to use these language frames to help you.
■ **Using a photograph, ask kids to turn and talk about what they learned and their reactions to the information. Explain what it means to merge thinking with new information.**	Talk about what you learned or your reactions. Then jot and draw this on a Post-it. When we combine what we already know with new learning, we are merging our thinking with the information.

Lesson 8: **Explore Nonfiction Features** *(page 37)*

- **Review the idea that when we read, the first thing we do is to think about our background knowledge.**

When we view and read about _____, we think about what we already know or think we know about _____.

As we think about our background knowledge, we can say:
I know _____.
I think _____.
I think I know _____.

That's how we talk about our background knowledge.

- **Ask kids to draw or jot their background knowledge.**

Go ahead and write and/or draw what you know or think you know about _____.

- **Explain that when we read nonfiction we learn new information.**

When we learn facts and information we say:
I learned _____.

And now try writing and drawing something you learned about _____.

- **Explain that when we learn new information, we often have a question. Model the difference between noticing or stating new learning and asking a question.**

I'm going to show you how I learn and wonder about information as I look at this photograph. I am really interested in _____ and I learned _____.
But this makes me really wonder about _____. So I'm going to ask this question: _____.

Notice that when I ask a question I can say:
I wonder _____.
I am wondering about _____.

- **Ask kids to turn and talk about something they learned or something they wondered about the text or photographs.**

Go ahead and turn and talk about something you learned or something you wonder.

Lesson 9: **Wonder About New Information** *(page 43)*

- **Page through the first few pages of a nonfiction text and ask kids to share what they notice about the text and photographs, as well as their background knowledge about the topic. Review and discuss vocabulary about the topic as kids share.**

- **Explain that good readers wonder about information and are curious so they ask questions.**

- **Model what you notice as well as questions about the photographs or the information.**

- **Ask kids to turn and talk about questions they have about the text.**

- **Ask students to share their questions with the group. Write them on Post-its and place them on the anchor chart.**

Turn and talk about your background knowledge about _____. Let's share what we already know.

When we are curious about something, we want to learn more. So we ask questions.

I'm noticing _____. I 'm curious about _____.
I have a question. I wonder _____.

I can begin my question with:
Why _____?
What _____?
When _____?
Where _____?
How _____?

I'm thinking about _____ so I'll ask,
"Why _____?"

Now it's your turn to use these frames and ask your own question. Think for a minute, look at the photographs and text, and then share your question with someone near you.

Now let's share some of your questions.
As you share them, I'll write them down and put them on our chart.

TEACHING MOVES

- **Introduce the text and ask kids to turn and talk about their background knowledge about a topic.**

- **Explain that when readers read, they often have questions. They read to answer those questions. Model a question.**

- **Model how you answer your question by using the illustrations, photos, or words in the text.**

- **Ask kids to try to view, read, and talk to answer their questions, and then jot or draw the answer if they found one.**

- **Emphasize that what is most important is to be curious and ask questions, even if we can't immediately find the answers!**

TEACHING LANGUAGE

We will be reading about _____ today. Let's take a look at what we notice and learn from the cover of this book about _____. As we look at the first few pages, turn and talk about any background knowledge you have about _____.

You all ask thoughtful questions. And sometimes the text answers our questions. Here's my question: _____. I'm going to keep it in my mind as I continue viewing and reading this page.

From the illustration, I think I can answer my question. I'll say "I learned _____." So I answered my question. Often we answer our questions by viewing the illustrations or photographs and reading and talking together. Notice how I can write my answer on a Post-it.

Now you try it. Turn and talk about any questions you have. Now think about if you can answer them using the text and illustrations. Or maybe you can talk to someone about the answer to your question. Go ahead and jot or draw the answer if you found one. Remember to use the language frame "I learned _____."

If you can't answer your question, that's fine. Maybe you will find the answer as you keep reading.

Lesson 11: **Read with a Question in Mind** *(page 53)*

TEACHING MOVES	TEACHING LANGUAGE
■ **Engage kids in the topic and support them to activate background knowledge they have about it. Introduce pertinent vocabulary.**	Wow, we are reading about _____ today! Pretty interesting! Turn and talk about your background knowledge on this topic. You are welcome to draw and jot your background knowledge. We'll put it up here on a chart.
■ **Explain that their questions are the most important questions. When we read, we often have questions. We keep these in mind and see if we find answers to them.**	You have been asking some great questions about the information you are learning from your reading. Remember that your questions are the most important ones. Remember to keep your questions in mind as you read. We will find some ways to answer these questions.
■ **Review language stems for asking questions. (See Lesson 9 for anchor chart.)**	Let's look back at our chart and review the stems, or words, we use to ask questions. Go ahead and turn and talk about any questions you have right now.
■ **Explain that we can use different features to answer our questions. Model how to answer a question using a feature.**	Sometimes we can answer our questions using these features. For example, I have a question: _____. Notice I used the questioning stem _____? to ask my question. From the (photograph, caption, diagram), I learned _____, so I used this information to answer my question.
■ **Ask kids to try asking and answering a question.**	Now you try asking and answering a question. Work with a partner and remember to use our questioning stems or language to ask your question. Then turn and talk about any information you find that answers your question.

Lesson 12: **Infer Meaning** *(page 57)*

■ **Introduce the concept of inferring by asking kids to infer different emotions from actions, facial expressions, or tone of voice.**

When we infer, we have to figure out the meaning without someone telling us. Watch what I do now. By paying attention to my facial expressions and body language, I think you will be able to figure out how I am feeling. [Act out being sad, or angry, or happy]. What you just did was infer from the clues you noticed. You used your background knowledge about people's feelings and the clues I gave you to figure out what was happening.

■ **Explain we infer when we read. We use text clues and think about our background knowledge to make meaning.**

We can do the same thing when we are reading. We use our background knowledge and clues from the words in the text to figure out what it means. We do this with _____ (poetry) because we want to really understand what the _____ (poem) means!

■ **Using a few lines of a poem or song, model how you infer the meaning of the words.**

Let's try it with _____ (a poem, a few lines of poem or a song). We'll read it together. Now I'm thinking about these words. I have background knowledge about _____, and combining this with the clues in the text make me think that _____ (share inference). I'm going to draw what it means right here.

■ **Ask kids to turn and talk about the words or phrases in a poem and their thinking and inferences about these.**

Now let's think about another line. You can turn and talk as you infer, or think about, what it means. Remember you are combining your background knowledge with the clues from the words to make an inference.

■ **Remind kids to use the language frames that signal inferring.**

As you infer, remember to use the language frames.
I think _____.
I infer _____.

Lesson 13: **Learn to Visualize** *(page 61)*

TEACHING MOVES

- **Explain that when we read, we often create mind pictures that help us understand a poem or other text. Share a line from a poem or song. Then demonstrate the pictures you get in your mind that help you understand the words.**

- **Ask the children to visualize and use language stems to describe the images they get in their minds based on the words and lines. Note that different people have different interpretations and inferences.**

- **Ask kids to draw or sketch the pictures they have created in their minds as they thought about and inferred from the words or lines.**

TEACHING LANGUAGE

Let's read these lines from _____ (poem or song). When we hear words from a poem or a song, we often create pictures in our minds from these words. Here's what I am thinking about this poem/song: I'm visualizing that _____. The picture in my mind is _____.

Now you try it. Think about the words. When you get a picture in your mind, go ahead and talk about it with someone near you. Remember to say "I'm visualizing _____." Or "The picture in my mind is _____."

Now take a moment to draw or sketch the pictures you created in your mind as you thought about and inferred from the words.

Would anyone like to share? Remember that we all create different images and inferences from the words. That's what's so cool! We may have very different mind pictures!

TEACHING MOVES

- **Explain that when we read nonfiction, we infer from pictures as well as words. By inferring about the pictures and creating mind pictures from the words we read, we more fully understand what we read.**

- **Explain that when we see visual features in nonfiction, we make inferences about these and learn more information from them. Sometimes the visual features give us more information than the words, so we need to really pay close attention to and think about these.**

- **Model how to infer from visuals, pictures, and photographs.**

- **Point out that sometimes the words and photographs or visuals work together to give us information. Read and view to infer information.**

- **Ask kids to try inferring from features and discussing what they learned with a partner.**

TEACHING LANGUAGE

Remember how we used our background knowledge and combined it with texts clues to make an inference? We can do this with nonfiction features and words. Right now we'll focus on the visual features, think about our background knowledge and see what we learn from them.

Notice that I am inferring from these visual features. When we see visual features in nonfiction, we infer from these and learn more information. Sometimes the visual features give us more information than the words so we need to really pay close attention to and think about these.

I infer _____. The words didn't tell me that information, so I looked really closely at the photograph and visual features. I'm thinking _____ and so I learned _____.

Let's read the words. I'm reading the words and they actually give me more information about this. So now I'm inferring _____ and I learned _____.

Now you try it. Work with a partner to view the features, think about what you learn from them, and make some inferences. Be sure to say "I infer _____" or "I think _____" as you tell each other what you have inferred and learned.

Lesson 15: **Infer and Visualize with Narrative Nonfiction** *(page 71)*

TEACHING MOVES

- **Ask kids to turn and talk about their background knowledge for the narrative nonfiction that is the focus of the lesson.**

- **Introduce or review any new vocabulary or concepts important to understanding the text. Discuss or sketch the meanings of some of these words or concepts.**

- **Explain that as we read today, we'll be inferring from the words and pictures in the text. We'll also be creating mind pictures based on what we are listening to, reading, and viewing.**

- **Model inferring and creating mind pictures as you read. Also focus on questions and what you learned from the story.**

- **Ask kids to infer and visualize as you continue reading. They can record their thinking by writing and/or drawing.**

TEACHING LANGUAGE

Today we will be reading about _____. Turn, talk, and discuss what you already know about this topic.

Let's sketch the meanings of some of these words on our big chart. Who would like to come up here and help to make sure we understand these important words and ideas?

As we read today, we'll be inferring from the words and pictures in the text. We'll also be creating mind pictures based on what we are listening to, reading, and viewing.

Notice what I do as I read these words and viewed this picture: I infer _____. Also, I visualized _____. And then when I read on and thought about pictures, both of these helped me figure out what was going on in the story.

As I read, I learned some new information based on my inferences. I learned _____. And I have a question. I wonder _____.

Now you try it. I'll read a bit more in the story and then will ask you to turn, talk, and perhaps draw or write your inferences and your mind pictures. When we think and infer as we read, we really understand the story!

Lesson 16: **Figure Out What's Important** (page 77)

TEACHING MOVES	TEACHING LANGUAGE

■ **Activate and build background knowledge about the topic of the article by asking kids to turn and talk about what they know about it.**

Today we will be reading about _____. Go ahead and share with someone close to you what you think you know about _____. Or maybe you have had some experience with _____, so share out any experiences you have had with _____, too.

■ **Read the text and model an example of a big idea that you glean from it. Explain why it makes sense to think about what's important. We can't remember everything!**

Let's look through the text for a minute. I'm noticing that a big idea, or an important idea is that _____. When we read, we want to remember the most important information because we can't remember everything we read!

■ **Model an example of a detail from the text, explaining that a detail is a little bit of information about a topic.**

Now let's think about some details. A detail is a little bit of information about something. I'm noticing that _____ is a detail.

■ **Ask kids to think about a big idea or detail and talk with someone about it.**

Now you try it. Think about what we've viewed and what we have read about _____. Talk with someone near you about a big idea or a detail that seemed interesting to you.

■ **Share out important information and details to reiterate the distinction between the two.**

Let's share out what you talked about together. We'll make sure we understand what is important information in the text and what are details, or little bits of information that aren't that important. But it is true that sometimes little details can be pretty interesting.

TEACHING MOVES	TEACHING LANGUAGE
■ **Explain that paraphrasing is a really important skill to have. When we learn information we say it in our own words, that's paraphrasing!**	When we read, we notice new information and stop to think about it. When we do that, we put the information and facts we are learning into our own words. This helps us understand the information. When we do this, we are paraphrasing—putting information into our own words.
■ **Ask kids to think, turn and talk about their background knowledge about the topic.**	Go ahead and turn and talk about what you know about _____. It's always a good idea to think about our background knowledge before we read about a topic.
■ **Read a bit of the article, look at photos or illustrations, and model how you paraphrase the information.**	Notice how I can put the information from this part (photograph, caption, or other feature) into my own words. I'll say _____.
■ **Use language frames to begin a sentence or two that paraphrases some of the information in the article. Model for kids how you do this: first reading and thinking about the information, and then saying it in your own words. Show kids the chart of language frames that support paraphrasing.**	I can start reading and thinking about the information. Then I'll put the information into my own words by saying: I think _____. I learned _____. This is about _____. This is about _____. I learned _____.
■ **Guide kids to read, view, and think about the information. Then ask them to state it in their own words.**	Now you try it. Stop and think about some of the information you noticed or learned. Try putting what you learned into your own words and share it with a partner. Try not to say too much!
■ **Model a response or reaction to the information. Ask kids to try responding as well.**	I'll show you how I respond to the information. I have a reaction to this information: I think _____.
■ **Show kids the "Steps for Paraphrasing Chart."**	Now it's your turn, share a response or reaction with someone near you. Here's the chart we'll be using to guide us as we paraphrase. Let's review it together.

Lesson 18: **Organize Your Thinking As You Read** *(page 87)*

TEACHING MOVES

- **Review language stems that encourage kids to identify facts and information, ask questions, and respond or react to information.**

- **Model how you react and respond to information, and then ask kids to try this. Model a question and perhaps something you learned to review these ways of thinking and talking.**

- **Model a question or what you learned first. Then ask kids to turn, talk and share a question or something they learned.**

- **Explain that when we take notes, we sort our thinking on the "I learned/I wonder/Wow!" note-taking scaffold.**

TEACHING LANGUAGE

When we read, we have lots of ways to talk about information. We can say "I learn" to state some facts or information that we learned. We've been asking a lot of questions and these are stems or frames we use to ask questions (point to and discuss the chart of language structures). And finally we can react or respond to the information. These are our thoughts, feelings, and opinions about the information.

Right now, watch how I respond or react to the information about _____. I'll say "I'm amazed that _____." I am showing how interesting this information is to me, how excited I am about it! Now turn and talk about your reaction to some of the information. You can use any of the frames to start your thought.

And now here's my question: _____. And this is what I learned: _____. I'll say "I learned _____." Now you try it.

When we take notes, we leave tracks of our thinking. We write and draw facts, questions, and responses. This is a way we can hold all of our great thinking!

Lesson 19: **Summarize Information** (page 93)

- **Review the idea that we can learn information as we read the words and view photographs. Ask kids to turn and talk about what they already know about the text topic.**

  Remember that when we read nonfiction, we can learn from reading the words and from viewing and thinking about photographs. Look at this cool text about _____. Turn and talk about any background knowledge you have about _____.

- **Introduce the language of summarizing on the anchor chart. Model something you learned from the text using one of these language frames.**

  Watch me as I show how I use these language frames to share what I learned from the article. I'll say, "As I read this and viewed the photographs, I learned _____.
  The most interesting things I learned were _____ and _____.
  This was mostly about _____.
  Notice I am putting the information into my own words. Remember that is called paraphrasing!

- **Ask kids to turn and talk and use the language frames to share something they learned.**

  Now it's your turn. Think about some of the information you learned and use one of the language frames to share it with someone near you.

- **Introduce the steps for thinking and talking about a summary on the "How to Create a Summary" chart. Creating a summary will take place in the whole group lesson, but going over the steps in advance will familiarize kids with the process.**

  Let's look at the summarizing chart right here. This is what we do when we summarize, or put all our thoughts together to tell about what we read and what we learned. These are the steps: We think about the information and put it into our words. Then we put our thinking in order. As we do that, we keep in mind that we tell what is important without telling too much.

  We'll be talking about and writing summaries in our lesson today, so you will already understand just what to do!

Lesson 20: **Read to Get the Big Ideas** *(page 99)*

TEACHING MOVES

- **Explain that when we read narratives, we use inferring, visualizing, and our senses to understand what is going on in the story. Depending on the text, students listen and view the first few pages of the story and make inferences, create mind pictures, and use their senses to understand the characters and story line.**

- **Introduce the sensory language frames, on the "Using Senses to Describe" chart. Model how you use these to evoke sensory images, sounds, etc. This supports kids to act out a part of the story if appropriate.**

- **Explain that visualizing, inferring, and using all our senses to understand the story can make us feel a part of the story, almost like we are in it ourselves. Show how you act out a part of the story to make the characters actions, words, and feelings more immediate and comprehensible.**

- **Ask kids to work with a peer to "become" one of the characters—using their senses and inferential thinking.**

TEACHING LANGUAGE

Let's read the first few pages. Wow! I'm creating a picture in my mind and I can use my senses to hear, feel, smell, and almost taste what is going on here!

Here are some language frames to that we can use to describe our thinking and feelings using all of our senses: It looks like _____, I taste _____, I smell _____.

When I read, I notice what I'm feeling: The words and this illustration make me hear the sounds of the story. I hear _____, etc.

This makes me feel like I am "in the story," like I'm right there along with the characters. Let's act out this part of the story. Who will help me do that?

Watch how I put the characters actions and words into my own words: _____.

Now it is your turn to talk to someone and become one of the characters in the story. What would you say and do? What are you seeing, feeling, and hearing?

Lesson 21: **Explore and Investigate** *(page 105)*

- **Explain that they will be writing and drawing about a topic they already know about. This is doing research. When we do this, we write, draw, talk, and share information on a poster. Share an example from previous work if possible.**

- **Model how to illustrate and begin writing information on the poster. Use the language frames to support the information you write on the poster.**

- **Ask kids to come up with information, illustrations, and features that they can add to the poster.**

- **Introduce the word synthesizing and tell kids what it means.**

Today we'll be doing research. That means we will be writing, drawing, talking, and learning about _____. We will create a poster together. On the poster, we can draw a big picture of _____ and then we are going to work together to add cool information that you know about _____ to our poster.

Watch me. I'll draw a _____. Now I'll add some amazing information about the _____. I'll say "I never knew _____." Or I could say "It's amazing that _____."

Now it's your turn. Think about some information you would like to add to the poster. Maybe you want to draw a close up of _____. Or you can label the parts of the _____. We're going to work on this poster and add our information to it. We will all work together to create one big poster!

When we put all of our information together to share it with others, we are synthesizing information—or putting it all together!

Lesson 22: **Share Your Learning** *(page 111)*

<table>
<tr><td>TEACHING MOVES</td><td>TEACHING LANGUAGE</td></tr>
<tr><td>

■ **Explain that when we share our work, we have a conversation to talk about our learning.**

</td><td>

Today we will share some of the great work you all have been doing. You have created such interesting [posters, poems, project, etc]. When we share, it is important to tell each other about what we have learned first. Then the rest of us respond to the researcher's work and we all have a conversation about it. Your responses are really important. We all love to hear comments and thoughts about our work. In these kinds of conversations, we are all learners and we are all teachers!

</td></tr>
<tr><td>

■ **A child who is willing to share his or her work presents it. Model your comments, questions, or connections to this work. Draw kids' attention to the language frames that can prompt their responses.**

</td><td>

Thank you for being willing to share, _____. [A child offers to share his or her work or project.]

I have a comment about _____'s project: I like the way you _____.

Or I can ask a question about _____'s work: I wonder _____.

And I can even share my connection: This reminds me of _____.

Right up here are some language frames that will help us think about comments, questions, or connections we have.

</td></tr>
<tr><td>

■ **Ask kids to turn and talk with someone about their responses to the child's work: their comments, questions, or connections.**

</td><td>

Now you try it. Go ahead and talk with a partner about your questions, comments, and connections.

</td></tr>
<tr><td>

■ **The child who is presenting/sharing his or her work asks for questions, comments, and connections and directs the share session.**

</td><td>

Now go ahead and ask us what questions, comments, or connections and we'll have a conversation about your work! [The child who is presenting and sharing asks the group for comments, questions, or connections and the sharing conversation continues.]

</td></tr>
</table>

Language Practices Index

Comprehension Intervention
Small-Group Lessons for The Comprehension Toolkit Series

"We created Comprehension Intervention *as a resource to provide additional support to kids who need more time and more explicit instruction to integrate comprehension strategies and use them as tools for learning and understanding."*

—STEPHANIE HARVEY, ANNE GOUDVIS & JUDY WALLIS

Created to follow each *Toolkit* lesson, the *Comprehension Intervention* small-group lessons narrow the instructional focus, concentrating on critical aspects of the *Toolkit*'s lesson strategy to reinforce kids' understanding, step by step. Approaching each *Toolkit* strategy lesson in a new way with new texts, *Comprehension Intervention* lessons lend themselves to a variety of instructional settings:

- By explicitly reinforcing and extending *Toolkit* lessons, these lessons are ideal for small, needs-based **guided-reading groups**.

- In breaking down *Toolkit* instruction into smaller steps, these lessons make learning more accessible for students requiring **tier 2 RTI** instruction.

- Infinitely flexible and targeted, these lessons help teachers increase instructional intensity, allowing additional time for **tier 3 RTI** instruction.

- Based on shared readings, which allow for natural differentiation, the *Toolkit* whole-group lessons are ideal for **special-ed inclusion.** *Comprehension Intervention* lessons then offer additional targeted small-group follow-up interventions.

To learn more or purchase, visit **Heinemann.com**

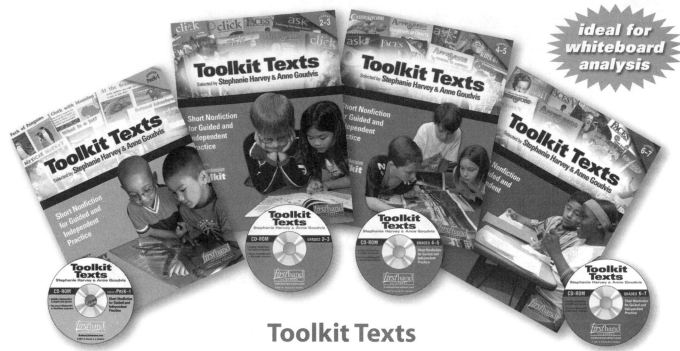

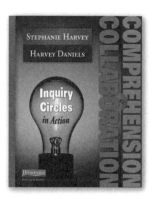
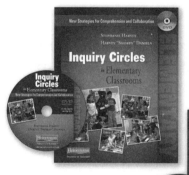